Praise for

I first met Annie Downs the summer she moved to Nashville, and I remember thinking she was the bravest person I knew. It's no easy thing to leave all that is familiar and comfortable to venture into the unknown. But I have watched God honor that decision and do more through Annie than I'm sure she could have ever imagined. Her willingness to follow where God leads is all over the pages of *Let's All Be Brave*. You will be inspired, challenged, and, hopefully, led to step out in faith to new places in your life as you read Annie's words and feel her cheering you on and reassuring you that God will meet you at every turn.

MELANIE SHANKLE, *New York Times* bestselling author of *Sparkly Green Earrings* and *The Antelope in the Living Room*

For years I've said that part of our job is to be brave and go first so that we give other people the gift of going second. In this book Annie did exactly that. It's your turn now.

JON ACUFF, *New York Times* bestselling author of *Start*

There are certain types of people who are capable of nudging us toward courage without making us feel small or insignificant, and Annie is at the front of the line. She is your favorite friend, the one who laughs at every dang thing, who tells stories you think must surely be invented (and yet they are not), and in the midst of it all, you discover you are dreaming new dreams. She has done that with *Let's All Be Brave*, and before you even mean to, you are putting your YES on the table.

JEN HATMAKER, author of *Interrupted* and
7: An Experimental Mutiny Against Excess

My friend Annie is a treasure, and her book is full of love, warmth, and courage. I can't wait to share it with so many friends so we can cheer each other on to the kind of bravery Annie is calling us to.

SHAUNA NIEQUIST, author of *Bread & Wine*

Annie is everyone's best friend. Imagine sharing coffee, amidst outbursts of laughter, as she stirs your heart to be brave. You'll walk away with new vision, someone cheering you on, and a skip in your step.

REBEKAH LYONS, author of *Freefall to Fly*

I've never associated myself with the word *bravery*. But as I read Annie's poetic, riveting words, it occurred to me that I've misunderstood the concept. For me, it was always BIG and DRAMATIC and FILLED WITH EXCITEMENT. It was jumping from a cliff into the water, conquering the heights — and sometimes that's what it is. But it's also learning to say no, and recognizing the way Jesus has gifted you uniquely for the journey you walk today. It's listening for His voice and stepping out in obedience and faith, even before you know the details of what's to come. Only a few chapters in, Annie had convinced me of something radically comforting — that being brave looks different for everyone, and there is every reason to believe I can do it right here where God has planted me.

ANGIE SMITH, bestselling author
of What Women Fear and Chasing God

Annie Downs is a comedic artist, a relational genius, and basically one of the bravest women I know. Her words sound like friendship and feel like courage, offering hope for those of us who want to live free instead of scared. *Let's All Be Brave* is fresh, relatable, and life-giving — her best book yet.

EMILY P. FREEMAN, author of A Million Little Ways: Uncover the Art You Were Made to Live

I am so grateful for Annie's voice and her courageous story in *Let's All Be Brave*. Authentic, moving, and completely relatable, Annie has done an amazing job of encouraging others to cast off fear and embrace an adventurous life of faith, bravery, and vulnerability.

NISH WEISETH, author of Speak: How Your Story Can Change the World and editor in chief of deeperstory.com

This is the book so many of us need to read. Finding courage right where we are is what will change the world. Annie Downs writes what she lives and believes, and we can feel it on every page. Anyone looking to grow in courage will be braver for reading this.

JEREMY COWART, celebrity photographer
and founder of the OKDOTHIS mobile app
and Help-Portrait

Annie Downs tells the truth better than just about anybody I know. In *Let's All Be Brave*, she weaves God's truth in and through her own true stories to make us think about what real bravery looks like. And while the whole notion of bravery seems to conjure up images of fairy tales or superheroes, Annie shows that real-life bravery is really a matter of whispering yes to whatever prompting God puts on your heart. Annie's beautifully written words, which are filled with humor, tenderness, and godly wisdom, will remind you that while responding to God's call requires courage, living a brave life is worth the sacrifice. *He* is worth the sacrifice. Every single time.

SOPHIE HUDSON, author of *A Little Salty to
Cut the Sweet* and blogger at BooMama.net

let's all be
brave.

let's all be brave.

Living Life with Everything You Have

annie f. downs

ZONDERVAN

Let's All Be Brave
Copyright © 2014 by Annie F. Downs

This title is also available as a Zondervan ebook.
Visit www.zondervan.com/ebooks.

Requests for information should be addressed to:

Zondervan, 3900 *Sparks Dr. SE, Grand Rapids, Michigan 49546*

Library of Congress Cataloging-in-Publication Data

Downs, Annie F., 1980-
    Let's all be brave : living life with everything you have / Annie F. Downs.
        pages cm
      ISBN 978-0-310-33795-9 (softcover)
      1. Christian life. I. Title.
    BV4501.3.D697   2014
    248.4—dc23   2014004153

Cover design: hand-lettering and illustration: Kristi Smith–Juicebox Designs
Interior illustration: Kristi Smith–Juicebox Designs
Interior design: Beth Shagene

First Printing June 2014 / Printed in the United States of America

For Nashville

This is another day, O Lord.
I know not what it will bring forth,
but make me ready, Lord, for whatever it may be.
If I am to stand up, help me to stand bravely.
If I am to sit still, help me to sit quietly.
If I am to lie low, help me to do it patiently.
And if I am to do nothing, let me do it gallantly.
Make these words more than words,
and give me the Spirit of Jesus.
Amen.

BOOK OF COMMON PRAYER

contents

a note from the author 13

an honest moment 15

just start 21

believe 33

nashville 47

edinburgh 57

your people 69

your talents 81

your words 91

say yes 97

say no 107

hold on 119

let go 125

at home 133

around the world 143

every day you have 151

everything you have 157

the why 169

the rhythm 177

jesus 191

good-bye 199

thank you 203

sounds good to me 205

a note from the author

I love writing in coffee shops. I love the hubbub of drinks being made and customers passing through, the conversations all around, and the smell of hot drinks and baked goods. So for each essay in this book, I've included the location where I wrote a portion, if not all, of that particular chapter. Think of me the next time you stop in at one of the coffee shops mentioned.

This book is full of stories — the ones I've lived, observed, and heard from others. I retell them to the best of my ability, as memory serves me. A few names and details have been changed in order to honor those I love, have loved, or could end up loving in the future. ☺

Annie Br

an honest moment

March 2013
My dining room table, Nashville, Tennessee

I'm not brave. I lack courage. I'm thirty-three years old, and I sometimes cry when I leave my parents' home in Georgia to drive back to my little brick house in Nashville. I have never jumped out of a plane, and I only ride roller coasters when I'm trying to impress a boy.

Some people live for an adrenaline rush. I live for a sugar rush.

I don't think it is fun to risk, to gamble, to possibly lose. I like safety, smart choices, and learning the easy way. Tell me it's a bad idea and I'm going to believe you.

A few months ago, my friend Lyndsay's car ran out of gas. (Something that does not happen to me because I do *not* let my gas gauge go below a quarter of a tank. I never once saw the "low gas" light come on in my first car. I don't know if it even worked. Never risked it.) But Lyndsay is a natural-born risker, and she pushes that two-door coupe to its gassy limits.

So her car coasted into Nichole's parking lot, and Lyndsay carefully directed it into a slot. It was out of gas, out of fumes, literally just rolling because the wheels are round. Before sitting down for dinner with Nichole, Lyndsay called her boyfriend, who brought over a can of gas. While she was still at the table, he filled up her tank with a few gallons of gas and then drove home. When she was ready to leave, her car worked fine.

Lyndsay told me the next day, "That did *not* hurt enough for me not to do that again."

She's the valedictorian at the School of Learning the Hard Way. And she wears it like a Ms. Tennessee sash and crown.

That's how risk takers roll. That is not how I roll.

But I want to be brave.

And I'm going to ask you to be brave too, even if you, like me, don't take to it naturally. I'm here to ask you to please do that thing in your heart that scares you to death. To make that move or leap or step or sound you wouldn't have made a week ago.

There is no formula and there are no rules. There is the Bible, our guidebook for all things, but other than that, being brave is organic and spiritual and a unique journey for each person.

I won't be making a list of brave things you should do. I won't be saying, "Here is exactly what courage looks like" or "If you want to really risk in a way that impacts the people around you, do these particular things." I don't think that works. I don't think you need me to tell you what to do. I think you know. I think you just need a little pregame warm-up. A little something to oomph you along. An understanding of the map you are holding.

———

I had lunch with my friends Chris and Jimmy this week, and we were talking about this very subject. And Chris said, "Courage implies action, like you are going somewhere or going to do something." Courage. Maps. Movement. We talked about what it means to be on your map and off your map and whether there's a map at all.

I left that barbecue lunch buzzing with hope and ideas. I love talking about what courage looks like (probably more than I like actually living it). I think an appreciation for brave people and brave moments has been in me forever. To this day, my favorite Steven Curtis Chapman song is "Burn the Ships" from way back in the mid-90s. It's a song about Spaniards sailing for Mexico in 1519, and upon arrival and in the midst of many hardships they wished they could go back. Instead they decided to burn their ships. Stay there forever. And figure out what that life would hold.

Brave.

That stuck with me when I first heard the song as an awkward middle schooler — sometimes you set sail without a view of the destination, trusting the tools you've got. And once you get there, you stay. You move forward, not backward. You burn your ships.

In my mind, when I think about you and me and where we are going, I see ships sailing and maps waving in the breeze and forks in the road. I see airplane arcs on tiny television screens and I see navigational tools strewn across a desk.

I see action. Movement. Travel.

X marks the spot, but it's not about the X. (Also, it's not about your ex.) It's about getting there. It's about the brave things you have to do between here and there to make you the person your X deserves. (Again, not what your ex deserves. You have got to get over him or her.)

But here's the problem: I'm known for getting lost. I cannot be trusted to lead if we need to get from here to there. So if you're on a journey or an expedition or an adventure, I'm going to get you lost.

If I had my pickings of what flaws to be known for, I'd go for something like "too pretty" or "too nice." Instead it's usually "too directionally challenged to be in charge at this moment." (Or any moment of travel, really.) Mama always said I'd marry a mapmaker — it would be the only way to balance out the deficit in my skill set. So any cartographers out there, give a girl a call.

I love maps. Before Siri would talk to me on my iPhone and tell me when to turn right and when to turn left and redirect me because somehow I had still missed the turn, I had a lot of maps in my car. I still have a few because, you know, I'm me and I get lost and I can't get too much directional assistance.

I need maps. And so do you. Maps of the mall because, seriously, I just need to pop into Gap for a breezy white cardigan. Maps of the airport because Atlanta's airport is practically its own city. Maps of your town and maps of your state. Maps of the places you've been that you never want to forget and maps of the places you want to go to.

Your life, start to finish, is a map. And we are HERE. That's all I know. I don't know where you've been and I don't know where your map will take you. I only know there will be moments when you feel like the map has turned or changed and moments when you realize you've read this map wrong all along. You will crumple it up and throw it down, only to return to it for direction once you finish your cryfest. I get it. I know.

But it's your map. Not my map. Or my cousin's map. Or your spouse's map. It's yours. And there is something so sweet about God doing life that way. Giving you your own rivers to cross and mountains to climb and forks in the roads of your life that I will never come to. You get to be brave right there, in each of those places. Bravery begets bravery. If you'll be brave, I'll be brave. And when I am brave, you feel like you can be too. We are holding hands and I promise I won't let go.

Let's all be brave.

just start

March 2013
Mountain Brook Starbucks, Birmingham, Alabama

I think the hardest thing about writing is the blank page. Or computer screen. It's said to be a writer is to have homework every day for the rest of your life. You remember that feeling, don't you? When you have a paper to write or an assignment to turn in and you know you can do it if you can just. get. started. I find the same to be true if I'm creating a presentation for a conference I'm speaking at or if I'm trying to write a message on a Father's Day card. I know what I want to say. I just often don't know where to start.

My favorite hamburger in Nashville is the turkey burger with a gluten-free bun at Burger Up in 12South. It's always cooked perfectly, and they have this honey mustard aioli that will just bless you. The owner of Burger Up is Miranda. She's a bit of a legend in our neighborhood for taking a boring stretch of street and adding some substantial eateries. I wrote my first book almost solely at her coffee shop, Frothy Monkey. Next came Burger Up and then a sandwich shop, and now? Josephine.

Josephine, the newest restaurant to situate itself on 12th Avenue South, hasn't even opened yet, but everyone in our neighborhood is buzzing about it. They're going to have a Sunday brunch that is pretty much all the permission I need to eat nowhere else after church except right there in one of her perfectly made booths.

Every time I run into Miranda on the street or in Burger Up, I ask how Josephine is coming along. She always tells me about another decision she has made — the style of patio furniture, the foods she has traveled across the country looking for, the right chef to bring to town, the kind of napkins and cutlery.

Every decision requires her to start somewhere. The menu was blank. The walls were blank. Even the title of the restaurant was blank. But one day she made that first decision toward offering us a new neighborhood favorite, and once things got started, they haven't stopped. Her courage shows up as community tables, delicious food, and warm hearts all up and down the neighborhood thoroughfare.

I'm flying to Minneapolis today. Travel is a major part of my life and job right now, which means fewer turkey burgers from Burger Up, but luckily, on an airplane seems to be where I get lots of writing done. Sitting in a window seat with my laptop open and All Sons & Daughters pouring truth into my ears — this is prime writing time for me.

As I'm buzzing over some farmland (I'm guessing somewhere in Iowa), I'm thinking about how hard it is to start, whether it's a new book, a new restaurant, or any other dream you may have. To start the journey toward that thing ... I don't know what it is for you, but it's not a journey *to* courage. The moment you take that first step, the moment you start, little seeds of courage, the ones I believe are already planted there right now, begin to sprout in your heart. You aren't headed out to find courage. It's in you, it is blooming, and it is with you as you travel and say yes to things that seem scary. Remember, it's not only the X that matters; it's getting there.

At my home church, the high school students host and run the middle school retreat. It's a really neat experience. As an adult leader a few years ago, I loved watching my sister Sally, an eighteen-year-old senior, be the retreat director. She nailed it. It was the only middle school retreat I ever attended, but I'm pretty sure she was the best retreat director *ever*. The coolest part about being an adult leader was I literally just had to supervise, not really plan or lead. It was awesome.

We were at one of those retreat centers that have cabins and bunk beds and two showers for every twenty people, and it was as rustic as you are picturing.

And I loved it. Yes, I absolutely love retreats. You know why? I love when all my friends are trapped in the same place for days at a time. Is that weird?

On the Saturday night of this middle school retreat, I crawled into my little twin bunk, shoved up next to another twin bunk, and closed my eyes. It wasn't thirty seconds later that I felt someone tap my shoulder.

Because we are a people who love to prank, I was

sure I was about to (1) be sprayed in the face with some sort of liquid or (2) get to participate in pranking someone else. Instead, it was Mallory, another senior helping lead the retreat. Because it was March, Mallory was just a few months from graduating and heading off to Auburn University.

She asked me to scoot over, so I did. I was worried — Is something sad? Something wrong? To snuggle up next to your leader in a twin bed means that something isn't right. So I lay there on my side as Mallory stared up at the springs on the bunk above us. Light from the moon barely snuck in through the curtains, but it was enough for me to watch as she was obviously wrestling with something in her heart.

"I don't want to go to Auburn," she whispered, and I heard the tears dripping onto my pillow. I waited, thinking she had more to say. When she didn't, I responded.

"Okay, Mal. You don't have to."

"I think," she stammered slowly, "I want to be a missionary. I want to go to YWAM." Her voice was still shaky.

"Okay, Mal. You can do that." I said it quietly. I wanted it to fall softly into her heart. Of course, I wasn't her parent or the final decision maker in her life, but I knew all that would shake out. She didn't need me to help her figure out *how* it would work out; she needed me to tell her that it *could*. I know what it is to need to say the brave thing, whether it actually works or not. To just start the process.

Mallory didn't begin her journey toward courage right there. That little glow of courage was growing in her heart for days, maybe weeks. And then in the hours and minutes before she actually got up out of her bed, it grew feet, didn't it? Feet that brought her to me.

Somewhere, at some point, she started being brave — probably before she even realized it. It wasn't when she told me. It was long before, when something in her heart began to beat with a different rhythm.

You just have to start, my friend. That thing that is whispering on your insides? That conversation you need to have or that place you need to go? That job you want to try or that ministry you want to attempt? That major you want to pick at college or that mission trip you want to go on?

You've got to start somewhere.

So do.

Tell somebody you want to be brave.

———

Today I volunteer as a leader for the college ministry at my church. It is one of the greatest joys of my life. I love that after four years of living in Nashville, virtually blind to the college scene (besides noting the massive decline in traffic during the summers), those students are now one of my favorite reasons for living in this town.

Each Sunday night after the service ends, we head together to the gym and eat cereal. Yep, cereal. College students totally dig it. It's hilarious. Our pastor, Pete Wilson, and I have a little game we like to play. We stand behind the cereal table and try to guess which cereal the students will pick. There are usually six or so options — the staples like Honey Nut Cheerios and Frosted Flakes and the classics like Cinnamon Toast Crunch and Lucky Charms, and then there are the wild cards that trade out, like Cap'n Crunch and Reese's Puffs, for example.

Here is how the game is played. A new young college guy will come over to the countertop lined with cereal and milk and supplies, pick up a bowl, and we'll introduce ourselves. "I'm Annie. This is Pastor Pete. What's your name?" And the startled student will say, "Uh, John."

I smile and continue. "John, we're so glad you're here. Now, Pastor Pete and I have a little competition going. We'd like for you to look at the six cereal options and pick the one you want. BUT. Don't say it out loud. Just think it. And then we'd like to guess what you are going to pick. You ready? Have the cereal in your mind?"

At this point, the student is usually quasi-entertained (because I'm obnoxious and Pete is really cool) and wants to play along, so he picks which one he would like — and we guess.

"Cinnamon Toast Crunch?" It's usually my go-to guess.

"Nope," John replies.

"Cap'n Crunch Berries?" Pastor Pete makes a left-field guess.

"Yep!" John says, and fills his bowl.

Now I'll tell you this, Pastor Pete has a pretty solid guessing percentage. But I'd like to have a formal investigation initiated because I am almost 100 percent sure that at least half the guesses Pastor Pete gets right are because the student changes his mind based on what the pastor thinks the kid wants.

And just so you know, I get about one out of every eight

cereal guesses right. Terrible winning percentage, I know. But they don't lie for me like they do for Pastor Pete.

Also, on a personal note, this is my favorite time of the Sunday night events. I get to talk to every student and connect with him or her week after week. As silly as it sounds, this is a big part of my ministry, and I love it.

Last week, Pastor Pete was out of town, so a new volunteer, Paul, stood with me at the cereal table. I tell Paul how Pastor Pete and I have this little guessing thing we do, and I suggest he and I try it for a little while. So we start guessing some of the students' cereal choices. I'm totally off my game and go 0 for 7 right off the bat, which leads to a lot of students rolling their eyes and my confidence going down the drain. Ouch.

Paul and I decide to take a break from guessing. We just start chatting as the students keep getting cereal — when, out of the corner of my eye, I see one of my college buddies, Will, mix Cocoa Puffs and Cheerios, and I think that is just a crime against all things cereal. I turn my head, point my finger, and say, "No sir, Will, that is gross!" Because apparently I believe I'm allowed to guess *and* judge cereal choices.

A few minutes later, as Paul and I continue to chat, he looks at me and says, "I don't know that I've ever told anyone this, but I think I want to write a book."

And there is the moment, right there among college kids and sugary carbs and inappropriate cereal combos. The moment when courage stopped bubbling only on the inside. The moment when Paul believed enough in himself and in the God who made him that he took a step of courage. He started.

I didn't plan to write books. Today's call to courage? I need to finish writing this book and be willing to write about some things I don't want to share but feel nudged by God to do so. But in 2006, when this whole journey began for me, it looked like eight pages.

I had to start somewhere.

The day I finished Beth Moore's *Believing God* study, I sat down at my computer and pounded out an eight-page document of my life as a storyteller — from a childhood full of exaggeration to an adult life of wanting to be full of truth but telling the BEST stories. I wrote about how God was revealing to me, through Mrs. Beth's teaching, that this was the direction my life was about to go.

God's brave moment for me that day in February 2006 was to write out what I was feeling with regard to sharing stories. He knows me. He knows you. He knows we need dreams in pieces because we would be too scared of the whole puzzle. Had I known I'd be an author and a speaker back then, I probably would have crawled under my covers and stayed there for a year or five. I'm here today because of the little starts and the brave moments dotted throughout my writing career that have grown into this.

I think of King David, way back when he's a kid checking on his brothers in the battle against the Philistines. When he gets there, everyone is scared to death of Goliath, this beast of a man who is fighting for the other army.

Young David the shepherd tells King Saul he'll go

against Goliath. Everyone is stunned because David is a kid and the rest of the Israelite army, full of adult dudes, is afraid of him. David's response shows us the importance of the daily steps of courage that lead to the bigger story.

> But David said to Saul, "Your servant has been keeping his father's sheep. When a lion or a bear came and carried off a sheep from the flock, I went after it, struck it and rescued the sheep from its mouth. When it turned on me, I seized it by its hair, struck it and killed it. Your servant has killed both the lion and the bear; this uncircumcised Philistine will be like one of them, because he has defied the armies of the living God. The LORD who rescued me from the paw of the lion and the paw of the bear will rescue me from the hand of this Philistine."
>
> Saul said to David, "Go, and the LORD be with you."
>
> 1 SAMUEL 17:34–37

And go he did! You can read what happened in this epic battle between David and Goliath in the rest of 1 Samuel 17. It's worth a read, even if you've known the story your whole life.

David, as a shepherd boy, fought a lion. And a bear. And rescued his sheep. He never killed the lion in preparation for the bear. He didn't kill the bear in preparation for Goliath. He just chose to be brave at every turn — to do his job and protect the sheep. And as the challenges grew in scope, so did David's belief in the ways God had uniquely created him, and more importantly, David believed wholly in who

God is and in the reality that David had a role to play on this planet that would require courage. Just like me. Just like you.

———

I've dreamed of this book for a long time. I want to tell two stories with my life.

1. God made you on purpose.
2. God made you to be brave.

In 2006, I wasn't dreaming of writing books. I could barely imagine writing out the story of how I wanted to tell stories! Then I started a blog that took courage every day to write. Then I wrote a Bible study for a group of high school girls who came over to my house on Monday nights. Then those printed-out lessons became *Perfectly Unique*, a book read by thousands of girls around the world. And then came my next book, *Speak Love*. And now we are here. You and I. And we are fighting against the fear.

My lion.

My bear.

My Goliath.

Oh my.

David wasn't done after Goliath. I am not done being brave either. Neither are you, I hope.

My prayer for you today is that you will open the eyes of your heart to the map and the next brave thing and the step you need to start. Tell someone your dream. Maybe even at the bottom of this page, or in the margin, you can write that first step. Make that first move to research or learn or pray about the thing that is like a God-struck match lit on your insides.

Maybe for you, it's writing a note. Singing a song. Making a phone call. Having a conversation. Composing a story. Writing a check. Booking that trip. Sending an email. Going on a date. Reading a book. Signing up.

I'm trying to list as many options as possible, but you know the thing God is doing in your life better than I do. It's time to get quiet before the Lord and ask him what it looks like for you to live a life of courage *today*. To start.

Just start.

———

By the way, Mallory didn't go to Auburn. She went to Australia with YWAM. We would often skype and talk about that day at the middle school retreat when God changed everything in her plans. After completing her course, Mallory came back home and married a great, godly guy, and now they have a daughter. They are missionaries in the Middle East. Every day they tell people about Jesus in a country that is closed to Christianity.

Just look at that. Look what her courage started.

And I can tell you firsthand that the moments of my greatest fears — those times when I was sure I was going to wimp out under the pressure of it all — have also been the open doors to the greatest changes in my life. So I step out, full of fear, but trusting that God is on the other side in new and wonderful ways. And so far? He always is.

believe

October 2012
12South Frothy Monkey Coffee Shop, Nashville, Tennessee

I have a lot of respect for tennis players. Tennis players like themselves a lot. They have a strut. A swag. They may play for a tennis team, but when it is time to swing the racquet, it's just one. Alone. Don't hear me saying they are self-centered. That's not (always) true. What I am saying is that tennis players are confident enough in themselves that they are willing to walk out on a court alone and win. Alone.

I grew up playing soccer. I adore soccer. I'm one girl on a field of eleven. I can play and have an impact, but if we lose the game, I can look around the field like, "Sheesh, girls. What just happened there?" Because, you know, it couldn't be *my* fault. Ahem.

I'm about to get my brag on. Prepare yourself.

I'm a good soccer player. In my prime, I could kick a soccer ball with a decent amount of power. Once in high school

I slammed one from center field that bounced off the cross-bar of the goal with a *ping* that could be heard anywhere on the field. Coach Moser jumped up and down like crazy. I remember it like it was yesterday.

It's not often that a coach celebrates a missed goal. So either he was the best coach in the world (because his enthusiasm obviously stuck with me) or he never ever expected me to score so he knew that moment was the best it was going to get.

We'll go with the idea that he was the best coach in the world.

I loved playing for Coach Moser because he always trusted me to make good decisions on the field, and he relied on me for strong throw-ins and stronger leadership. But when it came time to take penalty kicks, I didn't do it. He never asked. I never volunteered. (For you non-soccer lovers out there, penalty kicks are when one player takes one shot, unguarded, against the other team's goalie.) In nineteen seasons of team play, I took zero penalty kicks. Even though I would have scored. Probably. At least once.

I've never been afraid to be the center of attention, unless I can fail. Then I'm the one hiding behind, well, any-thing bigger than me.

Now as an adult, reflecting back on my soccer glory days, I can see the root of the problem. I didn't love me. I didn't believe in myself. I didn't think I could do it. And even more deeply? I didn't believe I could mess up and still be loved. I didn't think I could succeed, but I also didn't have the courage to fail. I had less confidence than any other girl on that field, certainly less than the goalie on the other team. So it was always team play for me — share the wins, share the losses.

But I'm not that girl anymore. I'm not the happy-on-the-outside-insecure-for-days-on-the-inside girl. The lies are gone (for the most part), and instead I see the truth of how God made me and who he made me to be. I don't fear failure because it doesn't define me. Neither do my successes. I used to want to hide in the moments that asked me to be brave.

Now I want to take a penalty kick.

———

My parents have a pond on their property, and all during my growing-up years we fished that pond. In fact, twenty years later, my mom still has the fish I caught with a jiggly plastic worm lure hanging on her wall. (I know. The fact that she still has that ten-pound bass from the 1980s hanging in the living room shows how much she sacrifices lovely décor and the respect of her friends to display her children's trophies.)

When Dad would take my sisters and me fishing, we had our own poles, oars, and life jackets, and we sang songs. I remember a song about a girl wearing a bikini to school, and I remember singing about Pete's dragon.

But the song I still sing sometimes is about an ant.

The song is called "High Hopes," made famous by Frank Sinatra. Apparently my dad wanted a fishing boat full of crooners. I'll summarize the song for you, only because I can't sing in these pages. (Honestly, anytime we are together, feel free to request the ant song. I love it. I'll sing it — you probably won't even have to ask.) The verses talk of animals that have to do the impossible, such as an ant that has to move a rubber tree plant, a large, treelike potted plant with big, waxy leaves. The chorus goes like this: "But he's got high hopes ... he's got high apple pie in the sky hopes." And then the song reminds us that anytime we get low and are tempted to let go, we need to remember the ant — "Oops! There goes another rubber tree plant."*

Ants can't move potted plants. It's just not possible.

But what the ant knew is that your muscles don't always determine what you can do. Your heart does. He believed in himself in a way I often don't. And because of who his heart said he was, he did things that were impossible. Courage is believing. Then courage becomes action, doing.

———

One of the beautiful things about Hollywood these days is that some people are sending the right message. While there is an overwhelming amount of godless, discouraging, and sinful images flashing before our minds, we do see a few glimmers of hope.

I like it when TV ads remind us to believe in ourselves and be confident we can do anything we want to do. You've seen the ones I'm talking about — an NBC star sits awkwardly on the arm of a couch and says into the camera, "You know those dreams you have? You can do them. Believe in yourself." And then the NBC "ding ding ding" jingle plays as

*"High Hopes," music by Jimmy Van Heusen, lyrics by Sammy Cahn.

a star crosses the screen. The more you know, people. The more you know.

Here's something I know: I shouldn't believe in me, at least not in the way they think I should. I've been me long enough to know that I am not someone to be believed in. I screw up. I hurt people's feelings. I care too much about some things and not enough about others.

I get lost. I am not perfect. And I don't want to pour my hope or trust into someone as faulty as myself.

So while I'm grateful for what Hollywood is saying, I don't think it is totally true.

I believe in the me God made and in the me God *can* make. I believe he made me on purpose and didn't make any mistakes when it came to my creation. I believe he is doing a good work in me, and in you. And that though I am flawed, God is loving me and refining me and reminding me that God in me is where I can place my trust.

And that is the place where I find my courage. It's like if you drive down This Is How God Made Me Road until it intersects with This Is Who God Can Make Me Avenue, there is a pile of courage waiting there. (I swore I wouldn't do cheesy map-related sentences like this, but can I just this once?)

The better you know you, the better you can find that intersection and the better you can resist temptation to sin or wimp out. I know my tendencies and fears, and I also know my gifts and hopes. It's where those meet that I often find God cheering for me to make the brave choice.

You have to believe in the One who made you. I am

confident in who God made me, but certain I couldn't do this life—or be brave—on my own.

God is perfect (we are not). He sees the big picture (we do not). He knows everything (we do not). So I choose to believe in this—that I am who I am on purpose, that the One who made me has a purpose and has unconditional love for me and those in my life.

I'm not saying if I had believed these truths in high school I would have been the highest scoring defender in the history of my school's soccer program. Believing God about who you are doesn't make you a superhero or an All-American athlete or a rock star.

But if I would have believed these things—really believed them at my core—I would have been brave enough to try. Coach Moser might have called on me for a penalty kick. I might have been willing to take a few shots. To risk failure. To just try.

———

I became a Christian at a very young age. Five years old. I grew up attending youth group and being really involved in every activity I could—from being in a small group to being in choir to working Mother's Morning Out in the summers.

Actually, we spent a lot of time hanging around Marietta First United Methodist Church in the summers. We'd bug the youth pastors, film videos for summer camp, hang out in the Sunday school rooms, play basketball in the gym, and walk to lunch at Wendy's. As a teen, my church friends were my best friends, and most of my favorite memories from that season of life involve those people and that place.

In all the teaching and training and time spent in church, at some point in my younger years, my theology got skewed and I started to believe that Christians somehow got ranked — not based on their sin or their bank accounts, but based on their calling.

You want to be a missionary? You get 5 out of 5 stars. Top notch. Cream of the crop.

You want to be a Hollywood movie star? You get 1 out of 5 stars because, you know, you'll probably be really rich and famous, and that just can't be Christian. Or you want to have a normal job at a bank? Okay, that's 2 out of 5 stars, because you can witness to people in the drive-through. Sorry you aren't 5 out of 5, but you are still *totally* a Christian; you just aren't sacrificing as much as the missionary. God still loves you so much, but you just aren't as awesome or something.

Every other job or calling falls somewhere in this range. My little confused Christian mind was sure that God ranked people like this. I don't know where I got this idea. It wasn't a lesson taught in my tenth-grade Sunday school class or something my parents instructed us on over dinner. But I remember how it felt.

———

My sister Tatum got saved when she was eleven. I was thirteen then. So I had been on the Jesus train for a while, but it was all new to her. And I'll tell you what, Tatum had one of those conversions where the old Tatum was really gone and a whole new Tatum was there. It was amazing.

And pretty soon after she got saved, she knew she wanted to be a missionary.

And suddenly, I was a second-class Christian. She was new and I was old hat. She was really brave and I was really normal. I wanted to teach elementary school. She wanted to live in a hut. And most likely, she was going to be really hot and sweaty in whatever mission field she chose.

I hate being hot. I always thought missionaries ended up in really hot climates. So I decided missionary work was not for me and resigned myself to the fact that I was never going to be as good at being a Christian as Tatum was.

I could work as hard as I could, maybe even get 4.5 out of 5 stars if I taught school in *really* dangerous areas or worked a lot of extra hours, but unfortunately, I'd never be at the top.

Just to be clear. My theology was super off, and this whole line of thinking is wrong wrong wrong. I see that now, but as an impressionable child, seeing certain professions celebrated repeatedly in the church skewed my view a bit. I don't think it was intentional, but at some point, a conversation going on around me infiltrated my thoughts and bled into my understanding of God and his plan for my life.

————

As I grew up and began to see Christianity with much more clarity, I learned a few things:

1. Not every place on the planet is hot, so not every missionary is moving to a hot climate. Noted.

2. If we were all missionaries, the world would not work right. Who would pray for them? Financially support them? Give them a comfortable home to return to after a year on the field?

3. God doesn't ask all of us to be foreign missionaries. He asks us to be us.

4. And who says what you are doing *right now right here* isn't God's work?

That's why we have to believe that God made us each on purpose. If we are each as unique as the Bible says we are, then our calls to courage are each equally unique.

Tatum's call to courage at one time looked like moving around the world and sharing about Jesus. My call to courage has looked different. For a while, it was teaching. For a season, it was coaching. Then it was moving and writing and speaking. And there are more calls to come that are specific for me.

But if I embrace them and step into them as they come, I can change the world.

So can you.

We each just have to be brave in our own ways.

Maybe you *do* want to be a missionary in a foreign country. My friend, that is brave. It really is. But so is being a stay-at-home mom. And so is being a counselor. Or a professional athlete. Or a writer. Or an event planner. Or a technician.

Courage looks different for each of us.

If we want to see God glorified all over the world, we need to be brave enough to see courage in all its different forms. And we need to do the thing. I can't see into your life to tell you what that thing is today — but I know enough to understand that the brave decisions you make at fifteen affect the brave choices you make at twenty-five — and they are different from the brave moments you face at thirty-five and fifty-five.

To see yourself the way God sees you is the first step in being brave.

If you are seeing yourself the way God sees you, then you can see your strengths and weaknesses. And you can see they are different from mine. You can see the unique ways you are wired and the rare combination of qualities and desires that make you uniquely you.

And you, my friend, have a unique call to be brave.

So when you hear me say, "Believe in yourself," this is what I want you to think about. Don't believe in yourself in such a way that you think you can accomplish anything on your own. You can't. To believe in yourself means to believe that God made you and there is no one like you, that you have a unique call to courage, and that you can do the thing that is staring you in the face. Got it? Let's list it.

Believing in yourself, as we want to define it here, is actually to believe:

1. God made you on purpose and unique.
2. God has called you to be brave.
3. God will equip you to do it.

To believe in the One who calls you to be brave is to

admit that you, like me, are prone to get lost and that Jesus is the way, the truth, and the life.

We're going to explore a lot of sides of courage. Like peering at some sort of kaleidoscope crystal, no two people are going to see the same thing when they look for a brave moment. God is that creative.

It's not your job to see the same refraction of light and color on the wall. It's your job to be brave enough to look through the kaleidoscope, even if what you see surprises you.

———

When I think about courage, I think about Gideon. The one from the Bible. (I don't know another Gideon, but I figured you might, so just to be safe, I wanted to go ahead and clear that up for us. You're welcome.)

In Judges 6, all the Israelites are misbehaving in serious ways — the kind of ways that separate them from God. The Lord gives them over to their enemies, and they are living in fear — hiding away and being defeated and robbed all over the place. Then the Israelites begin to cry out to God for rescue (classic move, Israelites, classic). God decides to show mercy and deliver them, defeating the other armies by using the Israelite army. And Gideon, this little unlikely guy, is about to have a unique call to courage.

Starting in Judges 6:11, we see Gideon threshing his wheat while hiding out in a winepress (instead of separating the wheat in a normal public place). An angel of the Lord appears and says, "The LORD is with you, mighty warrior." This statement surprises Gideon because, well, he's *hiding,* which is not your typical "mighty warrior" behavior. But the Lord tells Gideon that Gideon is the guy who will lead the army to save Israel from the Midianites. When he hears this, Gideon immediately starts explaining to God why he is the wrong guy for the job — his is the weakest clan and he is the weakest of the weakest clan. But God knows. God knows he's picked the right guy and tells Gideon as much. (You can read the whole story in Judges 6:11–16.)

Poor guy. Do you hear what he is saying? Gideon is the runt of the litter, pretty much. And the runt isn't supposed to lead.

But that isn't the way God works.

Gideon is a unique man with a unique call to courage. And if you keep reading, you'll see that God really pushes Gideon to be brave as he shrinks Gideon's army from a respectable thirty thousand-plus men to a mere three hundred men. How many on the opposing side? Judges 7:12 says they were "thick as locusts." Yikes.

You've got to read the whole story, because the way the Lord rescues the people and defeats the other armies using just three hundred men is totally fascinating. (Check out Judges 6–7.)

And our buddy Gideon? He leads them. The self-labeled runt, who was once too scared to even thresh wheat on a public threshing floor, was now the leader of an army — a victorious army at that. God believed in Gideon. It took some convincing, but Gideon began to believe in Gideon and in who God made Gideon. And then? In that moment? Gideon was brave.

God believes in you too. He believes in all the ways he

made you unique. He believes in all the dreams bubbling in your heart. He believes in your ability to take hold of the tiny ledge that is your next call to courage.

I believe in you too. I believe you have picked up this book for a reason. You want to be brave. In your middle place — I like to call it the "knower," somewhere between your chest and your backbone — you know you want to be brave.

You aren't the runt. You aren't a subpar Christian. You haven't sinned your way out of your calling, and you haven't lost your chance to make a difference for Christ.

You are one of a kind, made on purpose, deeply loved, and called to be courageous.

nashville

April 2013
Portland Brew, Nashville, Tennessee

           I'm a Georgia girl at heart. I slept in a University of Georgia T-shirt for more nights in middle school than I care to admit. I've been cheering for the Atlanta Braves since Dale Murphy wore the uniform in the 80s. My parents still live in the same house they built in 1980 on the property my grandparents have occupied since the 1950s. I grew up in Marietta, a cute little Southern town where the same guy has done my parents' dry cleaning for thirty years and the waitresses from Po Folks Restaurant came to my grandmother's funeral. You know, Mayberry kind of stuff, but with more cliques and monogrammed purses and high school football games. For me, my childhood in Georgia tastes like salty boiled peanuts and fresh-picked blackberries, smells like honeysuckle on the other side of the lake, and looks like Wednesday night supper in the

Family Life Hall of First United Methodist Church right off the Marietta Square.

When it was time to pick a college, I looked no farther than eighty miles down the road to my mother's and grandmother's alma mater, the University of Georgia. With lifelong friends studying there and my home church's youth pastor now a campus minister, it was a perfect place for me.

I graduated from the University of Georgia and stayed in Athens for three years after that. You would too if you knew Athens. I logged a billion hours at Jittery Joe's Coffee Shop and cheered for those Dawgs during football games like I literally was on the field. (I still struggle with this— being overly invested in sports games I'm simply a spectator to. So consider that a warning next time we are together on a fall football Saturday afternoon or at a Vanderbilt baseball game.)

I also stayed in Athens because our church in Marietta had gone through a majorly painful split the fall of my freshman year of college. Relationships were severed, and I felt church-homeless. Because of the nastiness of the split and because my family was part of the crowd that left, I was no longer welcome in the building I had grown up in and knew like the back of my hand. Unfortunately, I also didn't feel like a part of the new church that had formed in my absence.

I like to stay comfortable, and Athens was comfortable. I graduated and got a job teaching fifth grade in a neighboring county, but my life was in Athens — my friends, my church, my home ...

Until my best friend Haley's wedding rehearsal back in

my hometown, when Mark, a longtime friend and the youth pastor at the new church, leaned out the driver's side window of his truck and said, "Annie, I think it's time for you to move back home." It was almost out of nowhere, though we had discussed a bit how I missed home now that so many friends who had grown up there were building lives around that same downtown square.

He was right. It was time. I moved back to Marietta at the end of that school year. I was twenty-five, seven years out of my hometown nest, and now I was coming home. I was mature (self-described), single, and ready to put down some roots.

I bought a house. I invested in our local church by volunteering with the youth group, and I got a great teaching job at Woodstock Elementary School. Fourth graders. I loved the life I had built.

I'm sure it wasn't the perfect experience that I recall, but my mind remembers it fondly, and I'm okay with that. I was home to stay.

———

In October 2007, I started to feel something unsettled in my spirit. That's the best way I can describe it. I would pray and pray and never feel like I knew what was up, but I knew something was stirring. After weeks of this weird feeling, I felt like I had to really press into it. I couldn't handle the tension anymore.

In my adorable little house, I walked up the steps to my bedroom and sat cross-legged on my four-poster bed. With my journal in hand, I began to write. I wrote out a prayer, asking God to direct me and asking him what was changing. I sensed I was supposed to make a change. I felt it being whispered in my heart, but I just didn't know what that change was.

"Should I change churches?" I wrote in my journal-cursive, a more bubbly and expressive script than my everyday. I sat there, mulling over the question, not feeling like that was it. So I tried again.

"Should I sell my house?" Nope. That didn't check out with my insides either. So I kept listing.

I wrote about changing jobs, changing small groups, changing families (just kidding).

Twenty-ish questions down the line, I wrote, "Am I supposed to move to Nashville?"

And it took my breath away. What? Why would I even write that? I had visited Nashville for approximately twenty hours one other time in my life, but certainly hadn't ever been there with hopes or plans to *live* there.

While it was only a three-and-a-half-hour drive north from Marietta, the worlds couldn't have been more different. In my mind, Nashville was all country music and big hair and a neon-lit downtown. To be honest, Nashville didn't have any more descriptors than that because I didn't think about it. Marietta was home, and Georgia was all I knew.

I sat on my bed in my house in my town and knew I was losing my mind, and I knew I was right. It was a weird combination of emotions.

And with that, my prayers changed rapidly and drastically. While the listening and questioning phase was full of peace even while being tense, I was now full of panic. *"Please, no, God. Please, please, no. Don't make me do that. Don't make me leave my family and my church and my home and my friends and my life. Please. I can't. I can't do it. I can't leave them. I'm sorry I ever started this. Can we both pretend like this never happened?"*

It was about losing everything. I was terrified. I barely like to go to the bathroom alone — I certainly didn't want to move to a new *state* alone. To live in a place other than Georgia felt absolutely foreign and unnecessary. I mean, have you seen that orange Tennessee fans have to wear? I knew I couldn't bear it.

I told no one. I didn't utter a word. Maybe, just maybe, I had made the whole thing up and if I just kept quiet about it, the nudging and the whispers would go away.

So I secretly prayed for weeks. *"Lord, please tell me I'm wrong and I made this up."* I cannot tell you how many times I apologized for starting that prayer that day in October. I was furious with myself for not just ignoring the whispers in my heart until they went away. I didn't want the answer I had gone after. I didn't want it at all. I cried myself to sleep night after night as I thought through all the many things this meant — leaving my family, selling my house that I had only owned for three years, not being around to see my best friends' children grow up in front of my eyes on a daily basis.

But it never went away. That one question written in bubbly script gripped me. Nashville? Seriously?

It was November. I knew I had to teach school through

the spring. It wouldn't be until the next summer that I could move to Nashville.

By Christmas, I realized I needed to start saying this stuff aloud. First on a family drive to Birmingham, I told my parents through tears. To my absolute shock, they agreed. "That sounds like a God idea, Annie," I remember my mom saying. I wanted them to disagree, to tell me I was crazy, to tell me all the reasons it was a bad idea.

But they didn't.

On New Year's Day, I told my two best friends, Haley and Molly. We sat on Haley's living room floor as I shared the story, and thankfully they were on my side — the side that said this was a lunatic idea and I had for sure just made it up. "If you want to be a writer," Haley said, "can't you just do that in Atlanta? There have got to be a lot of Atlanta writers around." For a solid twenty minutes we brainstormed. And then we stopped and the tears leaked as we realized the truth. God was asking me to be braver than I had ever thought possible, and it was going to bring sadness to us all.

I think that was the hardest part for me, really. Realizing there were so many other people — family, friends, students, my small group, coworkers — who were going to be affected by this choice. I wasn't the only one whose life would be disrupted by my leaving.

Before I told the general public, I figured I should visit the city. People were already going to think I had lost my mind for leaving Marietta. They would really think I had fallen off the deep end if I told them I was leaving for a city I had never spent a full day in.

There was one married couple, friends from college,

who lived there, and though we hadn't spoken in seven years, I shot them a quick email in which I explained that I would like to visit Nashville on the Martin Luther King holiday weekend in January—but "don't worry, I don't want to *move* there; I just want to visit for the weekend."

(Now when we talk about it, Mandy and Kevin say they knew right away that God was up to something that could end up with me living in their town. Fine, they were right.)

The weekend arrived, and after my teaching day ended that Friday, I hopped into my little red car and headed toward Nashville. I turned onto I-75N off the Barrett Parkway overpass, and I wasn't even out of my hometown zip code before I began to weep. If I hadn't been sure before, that moment made me sure. The Holy Spirit filled that car, and I knew I was driving to the city where God was asking me to live.

I cried the entire drive.

Three and a half hours.

Now I know this wasn't leaving for a spot halfway around the world, but this Georgia girl would be moving farther away from home than she ever dreamed.

———

I never felt brave. I never had a moment of extreme courage or belief that this was going to be the best decision I had ever made.

I just did the next thing.

Quit my job.

Sold my house.

Packed my belongings.

Said good-byes.

Pointed north until I crossed the state line and didn't stop until I saw the trademark of the Nashville skyline — the Batman building.

There are so many stories, so many moments when God injected faith and assurance into my deflated heart because he knew I needed it. He knew I was just wimpy enough to back out without a few shoves in the months before I moved.

A kind email from a friend.

A connection to a Nashville resident through a mutual friend.

An hour-long car ride with my friend Gary, who simply said, "Move to Nashville. If it doesn't work out, move home." (Ah, Gary reminding me not to be afraid to try and even be willing to fail. "Take the penalty kick, kid," he was saying.)

Just a sampling of the tiny gifts God gave me to remind me to be brave.

The first Sunday in August, I loaded my car and my mom's van, and together we drove to this new town empty of friends and history, and she left me there.

And all of a sudden, it was done. The thing that had been in the front of my mind and prayers and worries was no longer off in the future. It was here. I was here.

No friends.

No church family.

No family.

No idea where the post office, grocery store, or hospital was.

No life.

I won't bore you with stories of the weeping and gnashing of teeth that occurred for the first weeks (okay, fine, months), but it was terribly painful.

Can I say this again? *I never felt brave.* I never felt like I had what it took to be there. But I had no choice. I had a new address, and it was time to live there.

So I said yes to every "let's grab coffee" offer, and I had met some people — Jason, another Annie, and Marisa particularly — who generously shared their friends with me. I made myself go to church when I wanted to lie on my bed. I forced myself to drive to the Kroger grocery store in my neighborhood when my car wanted to point to Georgia. I saw how other people dressed — way trendier than my former life as an elementary school teacher — and realized I needed to make some adjustments to my wardrobe of fleece pullovers and jeans.

I just did the best I could to live somewhere that wasn't home.

Day after day, I just did the next thing, took the next step, said the next yes. And God built a life for me in Nashville that I could not have dreamed up for myself.

———

Three years after that first prayer that led me on this Nashville journey, I turned thirty.

In the backyard of Dave and Annie's house, eight of my dearest girlfriends sat around a beautifully decorated table as ten or so guys from our community served us a delicious meal. Lights were strung from the trees, and my friend Skip moved from angle to angle, professionally photographing the whole thing. No detail had been overlooked. It was the most perfect party I've ever had. From the muted gold décor to the grapefruit and avocado salad, Dave and Annie created an evening perfectly built for me.

The plates were cleared and the boys stood on the deck steps and sang "Happy Birthday," and, being that tears are my go-to mode of self-expression, I just cried. I thanked them all and told them the truth. *I never thought Nashville would be my home, and I never thought I would have people who knew me so deeply. And yet, here we were.*

We cleaned the plates and cleared the tables. Within an hour, almost a hundred people had come through that backyard to celebrate my milestone birthday.

I had never felt so overwhelmingly grateful.

It was the perfect night.

Nashville now? Years after that moving day? It's my home in every way. I am a better Annie than I've ever been before — less comfortable, to be sure, but more confident. I know God better and deeper. I know myself better as well.

Moving to Nashville never made sense, but it was right. I don't know all the whys of Nashville, but I see in my life every day that the story God is telling is best set in this town, personally and professionally. I came to this city reluctantly brave at best, a total wimp in all honesty. When I first heard God about the move, I thought he was asking me to give him everything. And in many ways, that was true. But the truer thing? God asked me to open my hands, and he gave me the world.

edinburgh

April 2013
JJ's Market, Nashville, Tennessee

As a sophomore in college (and for most of my college career), I loved spending time in the offices of my campus ministry, the University of Georgia Wesley Foundation — it felt cool and trendy and Christian. (You're welcome.) A campus ministry is a church for college students set on a college campus, and with so many of my youth group friends also attending UGA, every day I stopped by that building was like a homecoming of sorts. Along the walls hung photos of mission trips from past years. One day, I stood in front of one of those pictures — a group of college students clumped together in a sunflower field. The sun was shining on their heads, almost making the curly blonde girl look like she was glowing. Across the bottom it read "SCOTLAND."

I had heard of Scotland. That was about it.

During a Wednesday night service at Wesley that fall —

just weeks later, really—the mission trips were announced for that school year, and I saw SCOTLAND as an option. *Yeah*, I thought, *I wanna stand in that field and take that sunflower picture to hang on the wall of the Wesley Foundation.*

It wasn't superspiritual. I knew the Bible said to go into all the nations and share the gospel (Matthew 28:19), so it was more about picking from the list of trips that would be offered for the interested students that semester. I prayed, I remember that. But there was no huge SCOTLAND banner flying outside my bedroom window or any other weird signal from the heavens on this one. I just knew I wanted to go on a mission trip, and that was the one that stood out to me.

So I signed up, and within weeks, our team met and started making plans for the trip.

I grew up going on short-term mission trips (one to two weeks) and I always loved them, but I never felt like I was going to be a full-time missionary. You know, I hate being hot and dirty, and my idea of camping is making s'mores in the fireplace . . . in my house. I thought missionaries needed to be tough and rugged and willing to live without the internet. That wasn't me. So this trip, two weeks in length to a British country, felt very Annie. I loved the idea of going to a place that was chilly and had Starbucks and spoke English and needed to hear about Jesus. There was a great need to spread the gospel and a great opportunity to partner with ministries already doing that around the city of Edinburgh, and there was the challenge of raising enough support financially to go on the trip. We worked and raised money and prayed and packed, and before I knew it, finals were finished, I was halfway through my college career, and I was heading off to Great Britain.

In May 2000, the plane landed at Edinburgh Airport, and though tired from travel, I wanted to keep my eyes wide open. We drove to the flats owned by YWAM (Youth with a Mission). The ministry base was in Leith, the northeastern seaside area of Edinburgh, and it was where we would stay. I took in the sights and the jaw-dropping beauty of the green hills and old buildings. We walked from the base to the docks and picked the only open restaurant for our dinner spot. I had rhubarb pie and totally hated it.

For the next two weeks, we spent time ministering in Wester Hailes, a poor neighborhood just outside of the city center (or centre, as the Scots spell it). Helene, the ministry director, spent time educating us on this unique community and gave us opportunities to hang out with them. We did VBS-type camps, Sunday services, and prayer walks. We got some time to sightsee, played Ultimate, and ate deep-fried Mars bars.

I don't remember the moment. I wish I did. I wish I could tell you right where I was standing or sitting, what I was wearing, or what scenery was in my view. But I remember what I said to God. I said, *"If this is being a missionary, I can do this. Because this place feels like home."*

And it did. Maybe it was because they spoke English — and my previous mission trips (to Costa Rica and France) were challenging for me in that area. Maybe it was the weather or the people. I don't know.

But when I left that country, I knew I would be back.

And then I forgot Scotland.

For seven years, I lived my life and did my thing and never thought about going back. There would be glimpses, moments of longing or hoping or something, but it was never long or thought out. Instead, I would hear something Scottish or watch a movie or see a sign and think, "I love that place."

It didn't take much courage in 2007 when an opportunity arose to sign up to help lead a camp for Christian youth near Glasgow, Scotland. So I went. And I loved every long-sleeves-in-the-summer minute of it. It also didn't take courage to go back to that camp in 2008. The only minute of sheer panic, when courage would have helped, was at the end of that 2008 trip, in a van, driving by Loch Ness. I had just been baptized in that lake, and we were heading to dinner. Tom Fraley, an American pastor and missionary in Edinburgh, turned around from the row of seats in front of me, looked into my eyes, and said, "Annie, do you wanna move here and work with us?"

———

I was literally five days away from moving to Nashville. When I got home from this trip, I would pack my final things and load my car and leave Marietta, the home I had always known, and drive to Tennessee to live there.

I said no to Tom. In that shocked and quick kind of way. Not now. Maybe someday, but not now.

But that idea never left my head. Every six months or so after that, as I settled into Nashville and built my life, the Fraleys and I would skype or email. Tom would say they were ready for me to come, but I would have just signed a lease for a new place to live or agreed to a freelance writing job that required me to be in Nashville. Or I would call to say I was ready to come over, and Tom would say I was welcome, but the timing probably wasn't the best.

I didn't really want to leave Nashville, but something still tugged at me. And I wasn't as afraid this time. Because here's what I learned from moving those three hours north of Marietta in 2008: When God tells you to be brave, he will make it work. It won't be perfect. It won't be easy. But it will be your story and your best story.

So Edinburgh didn't seem like the lunatic decision it would have a few years before, when I was still that Annie who lived in her hometown.

But nonetheless, because I am, by nature, horribly wimpy, I found a good middle ground to moving across the ocean. (You know those people who decide to move somewhere and sell all their stuff and then move and figure it out when they get there? Yeah, that's not me.) Tom and his wife, Leigh Ann, and I settled on a plan. I went to Edinburgh for a month and lived with them. I went in the dead of winter, when days are terribly short and flights are terribly cheap, to try the whole experience on for size. No mission team full of hometown friends. No short two-week stay. Just me in a foreign country for an entire month trying to figure out if I wanted to take this step.

I landed on a Tuesday.

But Friday evening on my way home from dinner at my

new friend Mary's house, I knew I was going to move to Edinburgh.

———

At the end of that month overseas, I came home to Nashville and took a few months to get things in order, sell or store my belongings, and eat a lot of Mexican food. I posted a map of the city of Edinburgh in my room and read over it, memorizing every street near my future flat and our church and marking where each of my friends lived. And then three days after my thirty-first birthday, three years after moving to Nashville, I cried in the Atlanta airport as I said good-bye to my parents and got on a plane that was taking me to a life I had only dreamed about and prayed for, never knowing it would actually have legs (or, I guess, wings).

But I knew it would be okay. I had seen, with the move to Nashville, that changing cities when it is God's idea ends up being an awesome idea. It isn't free. It isn't always easy. But it's a good idea.

And I was luckier this time. I already had people in Scotland I loved, thanks to previous trips and my month-long stay. Harry and Anne, a couple who live on the west coast of Scotland, are practically my family. Harry took me to my first real British soccer match (Go, Rangers!) and bought me a team scarf to proudly wear. I am indebted to him forever. Tom and Leigh Ann, the pastors of Crossroads Church, knew me and loved me well. This church they were planting was to be a place for university students to hear about Christ. They had created a church plant team of volunteers from a partner church. That team was made up of some folks who had become my best friends earlier that year—Esther and Harry, Leisa, James, Kenneth, Melissa—and I couldn't wait to get back to them and join Tom as a member of the church staff. I had a community I loved in Edinburgh, and I was eager to return home to them.

I landed in Edinburgh in July with a return ticket to Atlanta booked for Thanksgiving, the tail end of November. Thanksgiving is the one holiday that my mother insists we all be present and accounted for. In my thirty-three years of existence, I have only missed half of a Thanksgiving Day, thanks to attending the Macy's Thanksgiving Day Parade in 2009. (Don't worry. I flew home to Atlanta that afternoon to be with my family.)

The plan was that the November flight from Scotland would just be to celebrate the holidays and then I'd move back to Edinburgh long-term in the new year.

Edinburgh benefited from those lessons I learned by uprooting my life the first time and moving to Nashville. I moved into the Morningside neighborhood and began to live there like I was going to be there for the rest of my life.

I quickly learned to maneuver my local Tesco, the grocery store on the corner near my flat. I also learned my way around Waitrose, the Whole Foods-esque fancy grocery store, because if there is one thing I will splurge on, it is ingredients. I figured out the bus routes (after a major meltdown due to memorizing the bus stops on the wrong side of the street). I bought a cell phone with map capabilities, for obvious Annie reasons. I loved my Scottish friends like I was never leaving them.

I was happy. Blissfully so.

The fall in Edinburgh is beautiful and crisp and the days get short in a blink, but those early afternoon hours take on a golden hue that I've never seen before. After lunch one day in early October, I sat at the Starbucks across the street from the Eric Liddell Centre with just my journal, my Bible, a peach muffin, and a soy chai.

I felt totally alive. I felt more alive that day than I had in years. It was like every internal cylinder was firing and I was the optimum Annie. I began to journal, asking God what it was that was causing my heart to live in a perpetual state of pure, happy explosion.

I listed three things that were true because I wanted to find the reason behind this and hold tight to it.

1. *I lived in Edinburgh, Scotland.*

    If this was it, the thing that made me feel so alive, then my suspicions would be true — I was staying because it was the best place for my life and my heart and, to be honest, my body. I was getting so much daily walking exercise that I felt the healthiest I had in years. And I loved living there.

2. *I was single.*

    While I certainly hoped this wasn't it (because I wanted to get married and have a family), I had to call a spade a spade. It was a possibility. The fact that I was simultaneously feeling like the best version of Annie and also being single was a new emotion for me. I didn't feel like something was lacking, and that was worth noticing.

3. *College ministry was a big part of my life.*

    I had not spent time with college students since the year after I graduated college and worked at UGA's Wesley Foundation. But here I was mentoring and discipling and hanging out with college students on a daily basis, and I remembered how happy it made me then and how fulfilling it was now.

I looked through the list and asked God again, *"What is it, God, that makes me feel so alive?"* While all three of those things were true for me that day, and the combination of them was making me into the best me, I knew my next step was going to be determined by that list and the question I was asking that day. I had to decide one way or the other: Was I booking a flight back to Edinburgh after the holidays, or was my time in this city done for now?

And quietly in my heart, I heard, *"You can do college ministry anywhere."*

And I knew. I sat back in my chair, a little in awe, and said out loud to no one and everyone, "Oh. I'm going home." I know this sounds crazy, but it hadn't crossed my mind before — that I might not keep living there. But it was clear. I would go home to Nashville and find a way to invite myself into the lives of college students there, even though I didn't know a single one of them. I knew my church had some sort of college ministry, so I just hoped I could get involved. I didn't know how it would happen, but at that table as the sun set over Edinburgh before dinnertime, I knew when I flew home that Thanksgiving after working at Crossroads

Church for a semester, I was going back to Nashville. And I knew I didn't want a life without college students in it.

———

It was a painful departure, even knowing it was the right thing to do. It breaks my heart over and over again that some of the people I love the most are on the other side of the ocean. I tell people often that no matter where I am — Marietta, Nashville, Edinburgh — I am home and yet I'm not home. Chunks of my heart live in each city, and it won't be until heaven when everyone I love will be within reach.

Because when I left those friends in Scotland the day before Thanksgiving 2011, I knew I was leaving for good.

Today I don't live in Edinburgh. I live in Nashville.

———

Eleven years.

Eleven years and two months after that first trip to Edinburgh, the trip where my heart found a home and my knower connected with a land it seemed to have always known, my map pointed me there again and it became my literal home. An address on Mardale Crescent and everything.

I saw God in Edinburgh like I never had before. In struggles that threatened to shred parts of my heart, in friendships that felt lifelong (and are going to be), in visions from God for our ministry and for the city and the university students there. I learned how to lead from some of the finest. I made mistakes like I was paid to do it. I was more fiercely independent than I ever knew possible.

edinburgh

It broke me to move to Nashville in 2008, when I left Marietta and everything that was safe and hometown. It broke me into one hundred pieces and I saw them lying on the floor of that first house in which I lived on 11th Avenue South. I thought they'd never connect again. But they did, in better ways, in a mosaic that made me more me. But Edinburgh? It bent me. I didn't shatter. Nashville changed me in ways that made Edinburgh possible and more beautiful.

———

I went to Scott and Faith's house outside of Edinburgh city centre for tea one afternoon in September. Faith asked me about my story — what had me here and where it all started. I told her of that first trip to Edinburgh when I was a sophomore at Georgia, of Helene who led us and taught us so well, of how I felt at home. I had looked for that ministry, googling everything I could to no avail, and I said that to her. Faith's face lit up. "I actually know that ministry, and I know of Helene." I could have cried right there. Faith told me of Wester Hailes (I had forgotten the name of the high-rise building neighborhood) and told me how to make contact.

So I mapped it, only to see that my flat was less than four miles from that very place, the place where my first "world missionary" heart was born. And thanks to Faith's resources, I emailed Helene. I thanked her, mainly, and asked her to lunch. I wanted her to know I was there, in many ways, because of her. It was those first weeks in 2000, the ones that opened my nineteen-year-old heart to a people and a place that would both eventually be my home.

your people

May 2012
Portland Brew, Nashville, Tennessee

In the fifth grade, my best friend, Amanda, and I had an awesome idea on the bus ride to school. It was the morning of April 1, and as fifth graders and the top dogs at Nicholson Elementary, it was our job to pull off an extremely awesome April Fools' Day prank.

With the bus ride to school being only about twenty minutes long, it wasn't easy to come up with the most amazing prank ever. But we felt like we had brainstormed a pretty smart idea. Because I am the epitome of a rule follower, I decided that as soon as we arrived at school, I needed to ask my principal if it was okay for us to gather the four fifth-grade classes together to prank our teachers. Here was the idea: the principal would call all the fifth-grade teachers to the front office. Then we would all switch to a different homeroom from our own and put our heads down. When the teachers returned, *their own students would not be sitting quietly in their classroom.*

I know. The fact that this is the craziest idea I came up with should tell you so much about my rebellious streak.

The principal totally went for it (duh, I'm totes persuasive), and about ten minutes after I got to my classroom, the intercom summoned all four teachers to the office. Amanda and I, in homerooms across the hallway from each other, peeked out the door and watched as the four teachers turned the corner. We quickly shooed our classmates into other classrooms, and everyone actually carried out our idea — they put their heads down and sat in silence.

(I did not see that part coming.)

But a strange thing happened. Three of the teachers returned, and the prank was a hit with students and teachers alike, but *my* homeroom teacher didn't come back. So when everyone returned to their homeroom and the announcements started and we still didn't see her, another friend came up with an idea.

"Let's all hide," Nick said, "and when she gets here, she won't be able to find us."

There was one closet full of paints and paper and teachery things, and so the twenty-something of us ten-year-olds sardined into it. The door barely closed. But it did. And it was pitch-black dark. And when the announcements played the song "I'm Proud to Be an American," as happened every single day during Operation Desert Storm at Nicholson Elementary, we sang at the top of our lungs so she would find us.

To this day, it is such a fond memory because it felt like

"our" thing—our little class had pulled off a prank the likes of what Nickelodeon afterschool specials were made of. Nothing makes you feel connected to the people around you like singing at the top of your lungs from the lakes of Minnesota to the hills of Tennessee.

Bob Goff calls them capers, and I like capers, especially when they bond people together. Amanda and I, next-door neighbors our whole childhood lives, lived out many capers. We rode our bikes through the woods, ran an imaginary store out of her playhouse, and challenged each other to spring the highest off the diving board and into the neighborhood pool. And with her by my side, I always felt brave. You are my people when we pull off a caper together, whether or not it involves national pride.

———

I love my people. I could write an entire book on that, which probably means this chapter is going to be too long, but I don't care. I want to live brave. So I pursue opportunities and look for God's open doors, but I only can because I have people who love me and with whom I belong.

We all need that.

In February 2009, I had only lived in Nashville a few months, but I had managed to finish writing a book, make some friends, and blow through my savings. I was really poor—I mean, barely getting by, having to ask my parents for money, carpooling to save gas, selling-things-on-Craigslist poor. And so were a lot of my friends. That year, many of us were on the first few steps of our creative careers, and those first few steps look like shuffling in the porridge line with Oliver Twist. I nannied. I worked at a restaurant called The Local Taco. I took jobs I found online for editing or writing copy. And yet ends just weren't meeting.

My friends felt it in their lives too, and the most frustrating thing, especially in a town like Nashville that is full of young adults who have moved here on their own to chase their dreams, was that we all wanted to be together. We didn't want to eat at home alone, but we couldn't afford to eat out.

And so began family dinner.

Our Sunday ritual started out simple enough. Much like the classic children's tale *Stone Soup*, we all brought what meager things we could in attempts to turn out a decent meal. Jason brought a pound of ground beef. While Laura browned it, Emily chopped an onion. We boiled noodles and added carrots (thank you, Claire) and a variety of fresh garden veggies (from Joel, who is a famous songwriter, so he's rich enough to buy fresh vegetables). And with a lot of water, that soup satisfied us.

Evan makes the meanest grilled cheese sandwich this side of the Mississippi. Thanks to Betsy, who brought a block of sharp cheddar cheese; Marisa, who provided a loaf of bread; and my garlic salt, we all ate our fill.

I relaxed into that family spot like it had always been mine. And week after week, we ate together. An email went out each Sunday after church — "Family Dinner: Italian Style" or "Family Dinner: Everything Starts with an R!" or "Family Dinner: Breakfast Style."

There would be a flurry of replies throughout the afternoon as to who was bringing what. I would check in before my weekly Sunday nap and wake up with the typical end result: Joel was bringing something fancy, and I was hosting again.

It wasn't always a perfect setup. When you fill a family with young artists pursuing their dreams, emotions tend to run higher than usual (creatives are known for that) and people get their feelings hurt. There were times when friends got left out or too many people showed up but forgot food to share so there wasn't enough to feed everyone. But for months, our tradition lived. We made room for each other every week. We prioritized each other — with our time, our money, and our groceries. We managed our budgets all week long so we could make sure we'd have enough left over for the lettuce or the cheese or the burgers — for whatever we volunteered to provide.

There was a night in the spring when grilled chicken salads were on the menu. The lights strung from the corners of my back porch were making the whole night hazy. The girls sat out there and laughed as they watched the boys test the strength of the tire swing in the backyard.

I'm sentimental about 2009. Someone recently pointed out I am above average in sentimentality and below average in the ability to control my tears when feeling said sentimentality. Ask, well, anyone. But 2009 is so stuffed with memories of people and times together that it just gets me worked up. When I think back on those Sunday nights, I feel emotional. We started as a group of church-mouse-poor friends who just wanted the ability to afford to eat meat, and then as we worked and got better jobs, family dinners lived on — and we lived like a family.

That group of people became a weekly community for me — over Skip's tacos or Jason's grilled chicken or Laura's angel food cake or Evan's grilled cheese sandwiches (which are good enough to get emotional over all by themselves). Sunday nights fed my body and my soul.

But it was more than that. It was an incubator for little seeds of courage. Phil and Sonnie were having their first child, and we could talk about their fears on Sunday nights. Skip left his day job to pursue photography, and we could talk about his leap on Sunday nights. I was beginning a new career I didn't know how to maneuver, and around the table, on the porch, or on the sofa we could talk about it. And friends would generously give their advice or condolences or congratulations. Best of all, no matter how high I flew or how far I fell, Sunday night always came.

I belonged there.

I think that's what I need most to be brave — a place where I belong. And you only find that place when you find those people, whether it's singing about America in an elementary school closet or hovering over a warm pot of soup ready to feed twenty.

No one is brave alone. Every superhero has someone they come home to; every Bible character has someone they depend on. Jesus had his disciples and his family. Batman had Robin. Paul had Barnabas. Ruth had Naomi. The Incredibles had each other; Superman had Lois Lane. Moses had Aaron, Hur, and Miriam. Noah had his family. So we see modeled, even in the Bible, the truth that the bravest among us do not stand alone.

My two best friends, Haley and Molly, have been there

for me over and over again since we met as kids at church. Whether I actually was brave or a wimp in need of a hug or a Coke Icee, they stood beside me. We've walked through highs and lows — immense pain and worry and illness and betrayal and also weddings and babies and laughter and years upon years of every emotion. They have been brave for me and with me. I hope I have done the same for them.

——

If you think I'm funny, (1) thanks and (2) thank my dad. Dad is a lot of things, including very, very funny. We talk on the phone a lot, and we often share jokes back and forth. For example, if I tell a story at dinner with my friends and they laugh a lot, I will almost always call my dad the next day and tell him the story, including describing the reaction from the others at the table. I think because I am like him, I'm always convinced he'll think my jokes are funny too. (He pretends to, at least.) When it's time to hang up, he'll say, "Big kiss!" and the appropriate response is, "Little wave!"

I know. It's weird. And I actually *don't* do it, though my sisters are better people who tend to respond in the way my father requests. Instead, my conversations with Dad end like this.

Dad: "Big kiss!"

Annie: "Yeah, love you, Daddy. See ya ..." then I trail off into oblivion and hang up.

But there is another one of Dad's fill-in-the-blanks that I actually really like. He'll say, "Who loves ya?" — and then before I even have time to answer, he says, "Dada. Dada."

Now mind you, none of us have called him "Dada" in approximately twenty years, but it still works.

Why do I like that so much?

I think it's really nice when other people remind you that you are loved.

It makes you brave.

When you know who loves you, you know your safe places. You know where you can rest. You know where you can go when you fail. (I'm sorry if I'm the first to tell you this, but brave or not, you *are* going to fail.) Knowing who loves you also lets you know who you can trust with your brave ideas and who will hold you accountable to being brave but not being foolish (if you let them).

I had lived in Nashville for approximately twenty days in 2008 when I drove home to Marietta for a wedding. People had barely missed my presence, but it was like breathing again for me to be in a town where I was known and loved. The weekend flew by, and suddenly it was Sunday night and I needed to head back to Nashville.

I stood at the front door weeping into my dad's arms. I just couldn't go back. It was too hard, too different, too empty. "Okay," Dad said, "you don't have to. We'll figure out a way to get your stuff back down here and you can stay. We'll hire movers or something. We'll work it out. But is that *really* what you want?"

I knew it wasn't. I knew God was giving me the chance to be brave, and in some roundabout parental wisdom and hijinks, my dad was doing the same. I knew in the conversation that he was going to love me either way — stay or go — and that he and my mom would support either decision. I knew it was breaking their hearts to see me so distressed and sad. And yet Dad offered me a chance to be a wimp and offered me a chance to be brave. Where it might have felt better for all of us if I had stayed home, Dad didn't make that the only option. He could have. Many parents do. But he didn't. His words gave me a choice. His love told me to be brave.

Somehow I drove away that day. Probably because my parents told me I didn't have to.

You may already have a list of people who love you growing in your mind. Or maybe you're still spinning your wheels to think up just a few. Maybe today is a good day to figure out who loves you. Their love will give you courage. Maybe today is a good day to tell the ones you love that you love them. Your love will give *them* courage, like a deposit in the bank of the heart. I don't know how it works, the science and math of it all, but I know that love given is courage gained.

When I decided to pursue writing as a career, my friend Shannon told me about a conference in California called the Mount Hermon Christian Writers Conference. She said we should go together. I was an absolute newbie with no idea what I was doing, but if Shannon said we should go, I was going to go.

I booked my flight and my hotel — and then? Shannon couldn't go.

It was one of those phone calls you absolutely do *not* want to get when you are already feeling totally wimpy and like you want to hide and forget about the whole thing. But

I couldn't. The money was paid. I wanted to be a writer, and so I was going.

I knew no one — I mean, *no one*. But my friend Kathleen had found out that a blogger she liked was going — Melodee. So she sent me Melodee's picture and said, "Find her and be her friend."

I didn't have any better ideas, and Melodee's blog made her seem like a nice person, so at lunch on my first day alone at a writer's conference in California, I stalked her until I found her, walked up to her table, and pretty much asked her to be my friend. It was terrifying. Sitting with her were two other women who were legitimately Melodee's friends — Sarah and Linda. Also at the table was a dude named Brad, who had come alone — a pastor from Canada. They invited me to join them, so I did.

And for the rest of that writers' conference, a full week, we were inseparable. We were the Hermonistas. And we belonged together; we belonged to each other; we had people. Bravery and belonging go hand in hand. We sat together that week and told each other to be brave, while we ourselves were mustering up all the courage we could find. I bolstered them. They bolstered me. We found each other and told each other to be brave.

———

But how to find them — the people who will stand with you and hold up your arms or cover your mouth when you should shut up — seems to be the challenge. The people are easier to identify than you may realize — you just follow your path and look around, because the brave ones? They are the ones parallel to you. They are your people. Just like every other hobby — panning for gold or mountain biking or baking or book clubbing — you step toward the thing that scares you and you do it and then you look around. Those people standing beside you? They are brave too. They must be to be walking alongside you on the courageous path.

your talents

May 2013
Pearl Cup, Dallas, Texas

April and I met at Signature Nails, my
favorite local nail salon, where I was getting a manicure.
April is twenty-two and in my college small group, but she
is a working woman, our church's pastoral coordinator.
She's keeping God's people going to the right place at the
right time with the right things in hand.

Let me tell you about my nails. They are tiny. I mean,
like really tiny. And for a lot of my life, I bit my nails like
crazy, but in the last couple of years, I've pretty much quit.
I mean, I still bite them if I get supernervous. Or if I'm feeling superinsecure.

Or if I am editing a book.

But on your normal run-of-the-mill day, I've quit biting
them.

(I'm taking a bow right now because I think you should
be applauding me for mostly defeating a bad habit.)

And now I love getting my nails painted. They are still stubby and small, even on their best days, but I like to paint them. Ahem, get them painted. It's a good use of ten dollars every few weeks, I say to my budget.

When April arrived at Signature, I was still picking out my color. A gray? A pink? Something soft. It was almost summertime, and with beach trips coming up, I knew I wanted a color that would work as an optical illusion to convince people that I was actually tan.

(I don't tan. I burn. I'm a porcelain doll. I'd have been a hit with the fellas in the 1800s.)

I ended up with an Essie brand color called Baby's Breath. It's a creamy white that leans toward peach with a hint of shimmer. Pretty much, I wanted to purchase the entire bottle immediately because it is the perfect shade.

Alas, I didn't. I let some guy named Luke trim and massage and clip and paint my stubby nails while April sat beside me as Betty painted her nails a racy hot pink.

Afterward, as our nails dried under that weird blue light, I asked April about being brave. I stepped into my small group leader role and asked, "What part of being brave do you want us to talk about? Like, right now?"

"I want you to talk about how you figure out what to do with your life."

Oh sure, April. No biggie. And then I almost passed out because that seems HUGE and like the absolutely most necessary thing to be brave about and maybe I'm not sure how to do it. But I knew what I needed to tell her. The story came to my mind immediately.

———

A few months ago I was riding on a plane from here to there reading *Freefall to Fly* by Rebekah Lyons. (Will you please read it? You should. Please.) I was sitting in an aisle seat, which I never do. I'm a window girl. I feel like the difference between an aisle seat and a window seat is the difference between an airbus and an encounter with God. An aisle seat just guarantees you you'll get to your destination. A window seat with a view of the ground from a cruising altitude of over ten thousand feet shows you parts of God's creation that blow your mind.

As we flew, I devoured that book. Her writing is just beautiful. And then I came to the chapter where she writes about the parable of the talents in Matthew 25. A rich man is headed off on a journey, so he brings together his servants and passes out his money to them. (Interesting tactic. Let's see how this plays out.) He gives one guy five bags of gold, another two, and another got one.

The guy with five bags? He gets to work, and when his boss gets back, he has five more to offer him — ten bags of gold total. The servant with two bags does the same — he gets to work and brings his owner twice what he had. But the guy with one bag of gold just buried it, dug it up when boss man got home, and handed back that same bag of money, probably stained by the dirt.

The rich man is thrilled with the first two dudes — obviously — and invites them to celebrate and share in the wealth. He's less pleased with the third. Actually, he's furious with that one-buried-talent guy.

I read Matthew 25:14 – 30 that day. I had read the story many times. Five to ten (that was good), two to four (that was good), one to one (and that was bad). The NIV calls them "bags of gold," but many historical texts call them "talents." A talent is a bag of gold.

But then as I read Rebekah's book, she asked me to think about any talents in my life that I had buried. Like, real talents, the way we use the word now in our modern culture, meaning things I want to try to do with my life, based on my desires and skills and giftings. (The old bait and switch, Rebekah. Well played.) And then she said to make a list and write them down.

It took my breath away. I closed the book, looked to the right and to the left, and tried to breathe normally. I didn't want to do this.

To be fair, I've made a few brave career choices — quitting teaching to pursue writing, quitting a great job at a nonprofit organization in Nashville called Mocha Club to step out into full-time writing and speaking.* But there was a talent I had buried in my heart that I didn't want to bring up.

It's that thing you want to do with your life that you quietly google sometimes or tell one friend once in college or ask your mom about in passing once, hoping she will actually think it's a great idea.

I want to be on TV.

---

*Mocha Club is a community of people (utilizing a community-based website) who give up the cost of a few mochas a month to fund development projects in Africa. We work in five main project areas: clean water, education, economic freedom, orphan care, and health care.

I feel dumb even typing it to you, just like I felt dumb when I told my mom and my friend in college and why I quietly google "how to be on the Disney Channel" and then clear my history because if anyone saw that I would be mortified and probably make up some excuse about doing research for a book.

I don't want to be an actress. I want to host a television show that young adults love but isn't cheesy or dirty. (No joke, my stomach is in my throat just writing this. But it's what I want to do.)

At one time I genuinely thought everyone wanted to do this with their life. As an elementary school kid, I would practice my autograph in the steamed-up mirror in my bathroom after a shower. I would bike around our concrete carport and practice answering interview questions and interviewing others.

But as I grew up, I gently laid down that dream, slid some dirt over it, and stomped it down a bit, until it was good and buried.

And then, that day on the airplane, Rebekah kicked at the dirt and made me see it. And then she had the guts to ask me to pick it up and do something with it.

How dare she.

———

I went to a class once where the teacher was Seth Godin, business expert and bestselling author. It was a five-day intensive course called the NanoMBA. I learned a book's worth of knowledge that week, but one of my greatest take-aways was the importance of failure.

When I pitched an idea to Seth Godin about how to get more people to share Mocha Club with their friends, he looked right in my eyes and said, "And what if that fails?" I was like, "Uh … my life will be over? I'll be embarrassed? I don't know what I'll do?" And my armpits started to get sweaty.

He responded, "No, you'll be fine. You'll come up with another idea. This isn't your last idea. It's okay to fail."

I believed him that day. I still do.

Seth is one of the most naturally brave people I've met. He tries things all the time — some go really well and some don't. But he keeps trying because he is a creator and he is doing what makes him happy, and then he's sitting back and letting the world decide if it makes them happy too.

———

That conversation with one of my business heroes was just the prep I needed before Rebekah challenged me to find my hidden talent. (This does not necessarily mean I'm actually talented as a TV person of sorts. She just shook up the desire I had tried to bury.)

The fear on that plane? The feeling like someone had just caught me picking my nose or reading something inappropriate? It meant that something was buried. I had been busted.

And I knew it.

In Eugene Peterson's rendition of this parable in *The Message*, the master of the servants says to the first two, "From now on be my partner" (Matthew 25:21, 23). And that hit me right in the gut too.

What do I want most with my life? To be doing the things that partner me with God. I want to be his partner. When I look back on my life, the greatest joy will be to talk about the times I was partnered with God in what he was already doing. I can feel it now when I fall into those moments — the feeling that we are partners who are dancing together professionally and perfectly.

And whether the result is success or failure, I think the trying is what gets you a partnership. Neither of those two servants went gangbusters making money for their master. They just doubled their investment by the time he got back. I wonder if the first guy actually made *seven* talents but lost two in the process — so that when the master got home, he had ten to hand him, even if at one point he had twelve.

Maybe failure is in that story. We'll never know. We just know that those first two dudes did the work so they could hand their master twice what he had handed them.

Chew on that, y'all.

———

I have a small group of people who advise me when it comes to work and life decisions. I call them my board of directors, though we never wear power suits or sit at a long, fancy boardroom table. We usually sit at my dining room table. They have unique jobs that make them experts in areas in which I wish to grow. One of the members of my board used to work for a television station and has all the contacts one might need to begin to pursue this dug-up talent. So as we gathered for our most recent meeting, I made a list of our agenda items and lightly scripted "TV show" in tiny print at the bottom, almost hoping we wouldn't have time to get to it.

(Are you, like, beyond impressed with my natural courage? I know. Me too.)

(Sarcasm.)

We got through the meeting, and they could all see that last little line waiting to be checked off. So I spilled the beans. I lifted that talent out of the dirt and dusted it off and held it out to them with fear and trepidation. And for the next forty-five minutes, we talked about how to make that talent double.

And oh, am I scared. It sounds like work and it feels like vulnerability and it smells of getting in over my head.

But it also looks like being brave enough to honor the talents my Master has given me, whether I double it, triple it, or come back to him empty-handed.

"At least I tried?" I'll say, with questioning in my voice.

And I think God will call me his partner.

———

So what are your talents? Will you let me kick up the dirt at your feet a little bit? Will you stop looking over your shoulder like I've busted you for reading about sex in *Cosmopolitan* and look me in the eye and tell me what talents you've buried?

I'm not saying you have to be brave enough to even *do* anything about it yet.

Just be brave enough to say it.

And then? You won't have the heart to bury it again.

Here's what, and I told you this when we first met some

pages ago. You know the thing. You know what your call to courage is. As we grow in knowledge and understanding of how God made us, we also get to grow in our understanding of the talents he's put in our hands.

My television confession is more than just a random example. It's a challenge to you. I'm looking you in the eye and saying, "Hey, I dug up my talent. Will you?"

Will you?

Prove it.

your words

October 2013
My dining room table, Nashville, Tennessee

She was standing outside, leaning against the wall of the fast-food restaurant we always passed on the way back to our neighborhood. She looked upset, so I slowed down, and my friend Heather said, "Hey, stop. Something's wrong."

I turned into the parking lot and parked beside the girl. I sat in the car while Heather got out and slowly approached the teenager, who was on her cell phone. She was bawling. Absolutely undone.

I couldn't hear them; Heather just wrapped her arm around the girl and spoke and listened. About seven minutes later she got back in the car. The girl stayed where she was, still on the phone.

"What was that all about?" I asked.

"I don't know. She never said. I just told her it was going to be okay, that God loved her, and then I prayed for her.

"I don't even know her name," Heather said.

We got back on the road and kept driving, headed to a going-away party for a friend. Heather never mentioned that girl or that moment again, but I think about it all the time.

I wonder about that girl.

I wonder about the impact Heather had that day when she was brave enough to get out of the car and comfort a stranger.

I don't wonder if it mattered; I *know* it mattered. I know her courage changed that hurting girl. Our words always matter.

———

If we go back to the book of Genesis, where the world began, we see that God started it all with words. He spoke, and things became. Light. Land. Lizards. All with a word. And we are made in his image. We speak, and things are created.

He was brave enough to make you, brave enough to make me, brave enough to make humans who would all break his heart.

Proverbs 18:21 tells us that our tongues have the power of life and death. I see that in my life. I see that in my friendships. I see that in the memories of past things said to me.

If there are seeds of courage living in all of us, waiting to bloom, words are the sun and the water that cheer on those seeds to their fullness.

Last year, I pressured about ten of my girlfriends to buy a month's membership to a boot camp. We were going to get fit in April 2012 if it killed us.

(To be noted — it almost killed me.)

It was no regular boot camp. It was a boot camp outside at 5:00 a.m. about twenty minutes from our neighborhood. So each of us had to wake up in the early 4:00s and then go exercise before the sun was even up.

How I convinced these people to do it I will never know. But I did. And Monday through Friday we would carpool out to the middle of nowhere for squats and push-ups and running and sit-ups and other misery-filled experiences.

As the month went on, the teacher realized a couple of things about me:

1. I did not enjoy being there.
2. I am the class clown almost always.

So in typical teacher versus class clown behavior, she started putting me at the front of the line or calling on me to lead the stretches or staring at me all too often. I hated it. As much as I love being the center of attention, I do not prefer it when I'm exercising. *Leave me alone and let me do my forty squats in peace, lady.*

On one of the last days of the month, we had to complete an obstacle course. As was the case every day, I was the last person to finish. The end of the course was a sprint around cones while holding a weighted ball. I began, and the teacher ran beside me, absolutely screaming in my ears.

YOU CAN DO THIS, ANNIE!

DON'T QUIT NOW. YOU ARE SO CLOSE!

YOU WOULDN'T HAVE MADE IT THIS FAR A FEW DAYS AGO!

FINISH STRONG!

As much as I hate to admit this, it worked. Her words in my ear gave me the push I needed to complete the course, get in my car, and never come back to boot camp again.

Just kidding. I went back for the last two days.

Even when you are at your lowest, like I was in that last leg of boot camp torture, the place where you think no one can help, a kind word can go a long way to heal and to rescue and help you finish.

I sat with my counselor two weeks ago, and, as counseling appointments tend to go, I verbally vomited everything I had been processing for the weeks since our last meeting.

When I was done, she looked me straight in the eyes and told me it was okay to mourn.

"Wait," I said. "I don't think I agree with that. I think I'm supposed to be fine that this is God's plan and that I trust him and that he is working all things ..."

She interrupted me.

"The dreams you thought would come true in a certain time frame never did. You saw a life for yourself that you will never have. You can mourn that loss."

No one had ever said that to me before.

But I needed to hear it.

Kate and I sat down to a lunch of meat and two veggies at the local place that is just a short three-minute walk from my house. I told her how this one situation with a dude hadn't worked out at all, but there was hope over here and hope lost over there.

"I just really think it's gonna work for you one day, Annie. I do."

I needed to hear that.

I needed to hear that I wasn't alone in my joys and my sorrows. It was brave of them to say the thing—to give me permission and hope, and both of those conversations built something in me.

Your words matter. The statements you make to others, the ones that get planted in people and cause something new to grow, that require a little more courage? They matter. There are things that I need my people to say to me in this season of my life, just like there are things my people need me to say to them in their season.

For the month of October 2013, I chose to write about "31 Ways to Speak Love" on my blog, and October 17 happened to be the day of a post encouraging my readers to say a random word of kindness. I wrote it on a day when my real life was kinda spinning out of control—unhappy friends, scheduling mistakes, big meetings to plan for, financial worries. On my side of the screen was hurt and chaos, and yet I had to type and publish encouragement and normality onto the world wide web. So I did.

Not many minutes later, Adam texted me. "Random word of kindness," he began. And for about three more sentences, he spoke into my career and my life and reminded me why I'm here. The timing couldn't have been better or more godly. I swallowed the words like medicine, knowing they would heal and grow something in me.

"Gracious words are a honeycomb, sweet to the soul and healing to the bones" (Proverbs 16:24). And to say gracious words is brave. To speak life into someone else takes courage. Whether you are correcting in love, standing up for the voiceless, praying for the sick, or praising and loving others, your words are changing the atmosphere.

Don't be afraid. Be brave. Say the things that will speak truth and heal. Hold your tongue in anger or fear — those are the times when a coward speaks. But when the moment comes to say the gracious thing that will mark a heart forever?

Say it.

Speak love, and watch as beautiful things come to life.

Say yes

April 2013
Portland Brew, Nashville, Tennessee

Because I fear risk and being wrong, making big decisions can be a bit of a downer for me. Moving to Nashville took me ten months. Moving to Scotland took me eleven years. (I know, you're impressed. What am I having for dinner next week? I'll start toiling over it and praying for revelation tonight.)

But one thing I always knew without doubt? I wanted to teach school. As soon as my younger sisters were old enough to sit up in chairs, I was making them play school — taking spelling tests I created on printer paper or completing simple math worksheets.

When I became a Georgia Bulldog, early childhood education was the only major I wanted to pursue. All I had dreamed about was being an elementary school teacher and running my own classroom, grading papers and making students line up in order.

I'm bossy by nature. Being a teacher is a great outlet for bossy people like me.

Midway through my senior year at Georgia, right before I began my student teaching experience, Bob Beckwith, my campus pastor at the Wesley Foundation, came to me with an opportunity. Wesley allows students to stay on after their senior year as interns, an unpaid position, and Bob wanted me to come onboard as the women's ministry intern. I was involved as a cell group leader for three years and worked closely with other students in leadership positions, so I was already volunteering a lot of my time in the ministry. As opportunities came to lead and help with events at Wesley, I'd say the little yes to be a part of what God was doing on that campus. And now? A big yes was right in front of me.

My dream of teaching elementary school was in view, and all I had to do was fill out the right county applications and meet a dozen principals and pray to God that one of them would trust me with twenty-ish children's brains for 180 days of instruction.

On the other hand, interning sounded awesome. Many of my good friends were interning, including my best friend and roommate, and I had grown so much within that ministry that the opportunity to turn around and serve felt right too.

But it was unpaid.

I had raised support before for mission trips, the most ever being $1,500. God had made a way, but not without much panic, sweating, and checking cash balances often from faithless me. To intern at Wesley I had to raise $15,000.

Fifteen thousand dollars.

While I'm a big believer in trusting God guiding us to make decisions — survey the situation, get wisdom from others, pray for direction, and then be brave enough to step out — for this one, I knew I wanted an answer. I knew there was a right and a wrong, and I wanted God to whisper that to me.

Okay, to be fair? I wanted God to write it in the sky in hot pink because if I'm about to try to raise a gazillion dollars, I need a sign. Like a real sign. Maybe stuck in my front yard.

I toiled over the decision. I prayed. I asked for wisdom from trusted friends, my parents, and pretty much any-one who would slow down enough for me to yell, "DO YOU THINK I SHOULD INTERN AT WESLEY NEXT YEAR?"

It wasn't that hard of a decision. Now, looking back, if someone asked my opinion, I'd quickly say, "Yes, do it. It's just a year. You will learn so much. God will take care of you. No biggie" — these kinds of things.

But in my sweet little twenty-one-year-old heart, it was the biggest decision I had ever made — pursue my dream career that included a salary, or delay it for a year and make approximately zero dollars.

On a Saturday morning right before Christmas break, I sat in my comfy white chair that has survived every move of my adult life and still lives in my bedroom to this day, and I opened the Bible.

While he was in Bethany, reclining at the table in the home of Simon the Leper, a woman came with an alabaster jar of very expensive perfume, made of pure nard. She broke the jar and poured the perfume on his head.

Some of those present were saying indignantly to one another, "Why this waste of perfume? It could have been sold for more than a year's wages and the money given to the poor." And they rebuked her harshly.

"Leave her alone," said Jesus. "Why are you bothering her? She has done a beautiful thing to me."

MARK 14:3–6

She offered it to Jesus. Her heart, her sacrifice, and one year's wages.

I knew I was being asked to say yes to this — to give up a year's wages as an offering to Jesus to serve the college students at the University of Georgia and to minister to Jesus himself.

———

Saying yes changes everything. Walking through the door, agreeing in the moment. Sometimes it is just what is needed to show you the next big yes. I said yes to interning at UGA. I said yes to moving back to Marietta. I said yes to Nashville. I said yes to Edinburgh. I said yes to college ministry in Nashville after returning from Scotland, in a major life circle kind of way. Today in my Nashville life, nothing makes me feel more like the Annie I want to be than when

I'm surrounded by college students. Each yes led to the next yes that led to today.

It's the circle of life, y'all. And now I shall lift a tiny lion into the air. (Just kidding ... *Lion King* joke.)

We have to say yes. Even when it's scary or costly or unknown. We don't screw up by saying yes to the wrong things; we screw up by letting all the floats in the parade pass us by and never jumping on one of them for a ride to the end.

———

I stood in Rob and Emily's guest bathroom, getting ready for a date I didn't want to go on. I live by a rule that if a guy is going to be brave enough to ask me out to my face, then I will be brave enough to say yes, even if I'm not lovestruck in moment one. I've never been a boy (although I've liked a lot of them), but I've heard it is really intimidating to ask a girl out, so I try to salute that courage with a yes — the first time at least.

Rob was lying on the couch watching golf, and I was quickly changing for the date, having scurried from my job at Mocha Club and needing to be ready in about fifteen minutes. I switched outfits in two shakes of a lamb's tail and then opened the bathroom door to talk to Rob as I put on my makeup and put my four billion hairs in some sort of organized fashion.

As I continued to get ready, Rob asked me lots of questions: Who is this guy? How did you meet him? What did you learn from your online stalking? Why did you say yes?

Before the inquisition was over, I was crying.

I didn't want to go on this date. I had only stopped dating a wonderful guy a few weeks before, and "getting back out there" felt like pouring salt in a wound in hopes it would heal. My friend Dawn had set me up. I trusted her, loved her, and believed in her set-up skills, and she also knew my heart was in rejected recovery mode and hoped that coffee with this stranger would help.

So I said yes.

But it was breaking my heart.

It was a fine date. We had good conversation, and he thought I was really funny, so that always goes far in my heart. We never went out again.

It didn't help. It didn't heal. But it did build something in me — the knowledge that life was going to go on. I was going to be okay. And a little yes can be a step in the right direction, even if it isn't a leap.

Some would say I tried to jump on the parade float as it passed by but missed it just a bit and ended up with some scrapes and bruises from the asphalt of the road. But at least I jumped, and I knew what it felt like to take off, even if I didn't appreciate the landing.

My people have said much harder yeses. Moving to India to start an orphanage as a single woman, then in twelve years having adopted over forty children. Giving up your solo music career to join a group of unguaranteed success. Giving up the life you know as a single person to get married.

You've heard before that saying yes to one thing is saying no to all the others. It's true, I think. If I say yes to a sushi dinner with my Vanderbilt baseball players, I'm saying no to Mexican with my friends. If I say yes to a city, a date, a friend in need, I'm saying no to all the other options.

It seems that Jesus did that for us over and over again. He said yes to uncomfortable things — like being friends with tax collectors and eating in their homes. Like letting a "woman . . . who lived a sinful life" (Luke 7:37) break a bottle of expensive perfume over his feet in an act of love and gratitude. Like considering Judas one of his best friends, even when he knew, *he knew*, Judas would be the one to turn on him.

What's your yes?

I have to wonder if there is a question lingering out there in your heart that you don't know how to answer. It could be big, like a location change, a job change, or a relationship. Or maybe it is a yes to inviting one friend over for dinner, attending one Zumba class at the gym, or making one request for help. What is waiting for you on your map just on the other side of the next yes?

It's a powerful word. I venture to guess it is one of God's favorite words. He's always saying yes to us if only we listen. (My friend Brian told me of a book titled *The Gospel of Yes*. I read it, and I totally recommend it if you want to read all the ways God is saying yes to us.) He's about giving and restoration and love. Those all scream yes to me.

———

Some of you are naturally adventurous, and saying yes is your favorite thing. I had a friend recently tell me that the greatest thing in his life is getting in a car and just driving until he is lost, turning whichever way the car seems to want to go. He's a yes guy. He lives on his map, even when he doesn't understand every turn, and he dances freely when the music plays.

But y'all know that's not me. Yeses, in big ways and in small ways, are hard for me, especially when I can't see what is behind door #1. But it is the yeses that have changed everything. Jesus modeled that. We see it in our heroes of real life, like Leonora Whitaker, the person the book *Christy* is based on.

I think of Leonora and how she left her family and home in the early 1900s to go alone, as a young single woman, to teach school in the mountains of Tennessee. Long before phone lines, emails, or FaceTime, she said yes to a chance to educate those in need, even when it meant leaving those she knew and loved.

I think about when Dave Barnes said yes to putting his song "God Gave Me You" on Christian radio, even though that wasn't where his music had played before, never knowing that one night country star Blake Shelton would be driving through the back roads of Oklahoma, hear the song on the radio, and decide to record it, thus giving Dave his first #1 song ever.

Connor didn't know when he said yes to playing baseball in his senior year at Vanderbilt (instead of going to the major leagues when he was drafted as a junior) that he would have his best year on the field and off in Nashville, thus earning him a higher draft spot after his senior season.

Ashley didn't know when she said yes to moving to Kansas City to be an intern at the International House of *say yes*

Prayer that the man who would become her husband had done the same.

The groom says yes.

The pregnancy test says yes.

The college acceptance letter says yes.

The job offer says yes.

But will you? I hope so. I really, really hope so. I hope you'll be brave and say yes.

Say yes to the gym.

Say yes to the open door.

Say yes to the situations that stretch you and scare you and ask you to be a better you than you think you can be.

Say yes to the moments that will only come once.

Say yes to serving.

Say yes to Jesus in every way — every chance you get.

say no

July 2013
Portland Brew, Nashville, Tennessee

I'm terrible at saying no. To be fair, I'm terrible at a lot of things, but saying no might be at the top of the list. In fact, I have come to realize that if I say to myself, "You absolutely cannot have/say/do that thing," I tend to end up seeking/saying/doing it. Whether I promise myself I won't share about the text message a cute boy sent me and then immediately tell someone, or whether I'm trying to decide if I should stay in or go to a concert, even if I have to be up early the next morning — you better believe I'm at the concert — because I just don't like to say no.

But brave people learn to say no.

Most people wouldn't think of saying no as a quality of someone brave. Saying yes is certainly the more heralded option, but sometimes saying no can be the tougher choice by far.

———

I'm overweight. I don't like talking about it. It has been a fact since the fourth grade, it's something I struggle with pretty much every day, and if I talk about it, it makes it more real or a bigger deal or something. I don't know. I just know it makes me sad and mad.

I've been on a diet, or wanting to be on a diet, since I was in the sixth grade. For those of you who keep calculations at home, that is approximately twenty-one-plus years at this point. More than two-thirds of my life.

Gosh. That's staggering to realize. What a waste.

In 2003, I was diagnosed with polycystic ovary syndrome (PCOS). Among some other really lovely side effects, PCOS makes it difficult to lose weight, process insulin correctly, and have a regular period. In fact, according to the website WomensHealth.gov, as many as one in ten women could have PCOS, so you may be sitting next to someone in class or church or passing someone in the grocery store aisle who is struggling just like me.

If you're in the grocery store, she's the one wishing her cart was full of muffins instead of veggies. Look into her eyes. You will know.

I spent most of my adolescent years thinking that because I was treating my body badly, it didn't work right in many areas. But it ended up I had a disease working against me as well.

Don't get me wrong; I also didn't eat well. It was a fairly regular Friday night in tenth grade when I would go to *say no*

Arby's with some football player friends and managers (I was a manager ...), and I would order — get ready for it —

1. large roast beef sandwich with liquid cheddar
2. large curly fries with more of that liquid cheddar
3. large Coke
4. medium Jamocha shake

And no kidding, I thought nothing of it. The more shocking truth? It is only the tiny shreds of self-control I possess that keep me from still thinking that meal would be a good idea. Would it taste good? Totally. Would it ruin my soul? Possibly.

(Just kidding. Sorta.)

Speaking of my soul, I thought food fed it. The places that felt empty in me, I filled with food. Lonely? Eat. Sad? Eat. Celebrate? Eat.

Yes, yes, yes. Never say no. Never deny yourself. Eat, eat, eat.

Why not just say no? Why not just eat less and move more? Why not just up my discipline and lower my intake?

I just was never good at it. That's the most honest answer I can come up with. I tried and failed and tried and failed, and because I wasn't diagnosed with PCOS as a teenager, I would try and fail, and the cycle of doing all I knew to do and it not working at all made for lots of frustration.

Repeated failure can really make you skittish to try again, can't it? It's true in relationships; it's true in *American Idol* tryouts; and it is true for me in healthy living.

It seemed that no matter how hard I worked in high

school and college to lose weight and appreciate my body, it never worked. It just plain never worked. And so I lost the courage to try again.

What for? Deny myself delicious treats for long periods of time to still wear the same size pants and still dislike my form? Yeah, no thanks.

Being diagnosed with PCOS felt like a light at the end of the tunnel. *So this is why I can't get skinny*, I thought, *and this is why I hate my body.* And yet for years after this diagnosis, while God changed my heart toward how I felt about myself, my habits didn't change. My eating didn't change. And my body didn't change.

I only cared about me and what I wanted. I wanted to say yes to all the things and no to none of the things, and I didn't care that it was hurting my body.

You see, the biggest side effect of PCOS is infertility. And guess what? I'm not sleeping with anybody. I certainly wasn't sleeping with anybody in hopes of procreating. So I didn't care that poor eating habits and lack of exercise were contributing to PCOS continuing to rage against my systems.

Yeah, I was unhealthy, but I had tried and tried to diet, always failed, and hated saying no to myself and the things I wanted.

Until January 2013.

The girls and I got up early on a Saturday morning and headed to a new (to us) brunch spot called Garden Brunch Café, located in what some would call the "less attractive" part of Germantown. We sat at a table for six and ordered mimosas and coffees and soda waters all around.

Looking over the menu, it didn't take me long to zero in on bananas Foster pancakes. I have a thing for pancakes and bananas independent of each other, so the idea that they would be combined was a blessing I did not know how to prepare for.

Our food came, and I surveyed the table. There were a variety of meals served, including other pancakes (amen) and grits and omelets and sausage and fruit. On the opposite end from where I was sitting, Kelley had ordered salmon. For brunch.

I shook my head in a "bless her heart but I'm glad I don't live like that" kind of way. As I dove into my sugary, fruity pile of beautiful carbohydrates, Laura asked Kelley why the salmon.

Kelley started into a story I hadn't heard before. I knew she had multiple sclerosis, and I knew the severity the diagnosis carried. But then she began talking about her progressing symptoms and how her fingers and toes had been becoming numb more often than ever before. She said she had changed her diet, saying no to a lot of things at her doctor's recommendation in hopes that cleaner eating would heal her body.

And it had.

The symptoms and numbness had subsided.

You know in Acts 9 when it talks about something like scales falling from Saul's eyes and he realized he saw Jesus and believed? Yeah, that happened to me.

I had a God-given moment of clarity when the scales fell from my eyes and I realized all the yeses I was saying to unhealthy food were inadvertently saying noes to the things I wanted more in my life — like a healthy future.

Right there, hovering over a plate of bananas Foster pancakes (which I practically licked clean because I knew things were about to change), I decided to say the brave noes that had always scared me.

Saying yes to feeding my body the foods it needs meant saying no to feeding my body the things it craved, and if you don't think that took courage, you have never dealt with addiction or seen me at a buffet of pastries.

———

I think one of the biggest mistakes Christians make while reading the Bible is forgetting that none of the characters, except Jesus, knew how things were going to end. So we read about Noah and immediately picture the rainbow. We focus on the fact that Jonah got puked out of the whale while forgetting he didn't know that was coming. We think of the disciples and the miracles they saw, like the feeding of thousands of people with just a little bread and fish, and forget they didn't know that story would turn out so awesome.

It did though, didn't it?

I try to think a lot about how much the people in the Bible didn't know. With that filter in place, we can identify courage much easier in the face of the unknown.

I am deeply moved by the story of Shadrach, Meshach, and Abednego in Daniel 3. These dudes were Israelites who were captured as slaves when they were mere teenagers and taken to Babylon with Daniel.

We see them say no to meats and rich foods for ten days in Daniel 1, and at the end of it, they are honored for their strength, especially in the face of eating much less than the other soldiers in training. Later, they are honored by King Nebuchadnezzar, who gives them important roles in his service. The king likes these guys. He thinks they are smart and strong and beneficial to his kingdom.

Years later, our boys are administrators over all of Babylon, and Daniel is serving at the royal court. (Quite a move from being captive teenagers, huh?) King Nebuchadnezzar builds a massive gold statue — ninety feet high, nine feet wide (Daniel 3). That's like what? A very skinny seven-story building? Gracious. And then he decides that everyone in town has to bow to the statue and worship it whenever the music plays, and anyone who doesn't will be thrown into a blazing furnace.

So. He's an extremist. I get it.

Our guys — Shadrach, Meshach, and Abednego — worship the one true God and have no interest in bowing to anything else. They say no when the rest of the people say yes. They don't bow when everyone else does.

Can you imagine that courage? To stand when everyone else bows? Knowing the result, knowing who you are and how much you are respected and yet choosing to go against your boss, namely, *the king*, in a life-threatening way?

That's a major no that risked everything.

But that's not the part that moves me.

When they are tattled on for not bowing and are brought before the king, he is furious. Like, whoa furious. Like, "You are my top dudes and you gotta do what I say" kind of furious. Like when the oldest kid in a family doesn't follow the rules and it makes the parents extra-mad because the younger ones are seeing it? Yeah, that.

Let's pick it up in verse 13 of Daniel 3.

> Furious, King Nebuchadnezzar ordered Shadrach, Meshach, and Abednego to be brought in. When the men were brought in, Nebuchadnezzar asked, "Is it true, Shadrach, Meshach, and Abednego, that you don't respect my gods and refuse to worship the gold statue that I have set up? I'm giving you a second chance—but from now on, when the big band strikes up you must go to your knees and worship the statue I have made. If you don't worship it, you will be pitched into a roaring furnace, no questions asked. Who is the god who can rescue you from my power?"
>
> Shadrach, Meshach, and Abednego answered King Nebuchadnezzar, "Your threat means nothing to us. If you throw us in the fire, the God we serve can rescue us from your roaring furnace and anything else you might cook up, O king. *But even if he doesn't, it wouldn't make a bit of difference, O king.* We still wouldn't serve your gods or worship the gold statue you set up."
>
> DANIEL 3:13–18 MSG, emphasis added

Even if he does not.

Even if God doesn't rescue us from this, we still say no.

They say a brave no; the king says he is going to kill them. They still refuse. Oh, I want to see this scene played back on the big screen when we get to heaven. I want to see their faces and hear their voices. I wonder if they shook.

I wonder if they were shoulder to shoulder, pressing into each other for strength. I wonder who actually spoke up.

And whoever said it said the thing I hope I always have the courage to say.

I know what God *can* do, but even if he doesn't, I still won't worship idols. I will still worship the one true God.

The boys didn't question God's character or strength. They didn't serve God because of what he did for them; they served God because he's God. They were brave because of who God is, not because of what he could do for them.

I know God can heal my friend's illness, but even if he doesn't . . .

I know God can fix relationships, but even if he doesn't . . .

I know God can provide a husband, but even if he doesn't . . .

I know God can provide for me financially, but even if he doesn't . . .

I know God can answer this prayer, but even if he doesn't . . .

I know God can help us get pregnant, but even if he doesn't . . .

I know God can rescue us, but even if he doesn't . . .

I know God can heal my body and make it possible for me to have children, as I feed it what it needs and say no to the things that make me more sick, but even if he doesn't . . .

Right? EVEN. IF. HE. DOES. NOT.

Can you say that? Can you say it and mean it? Can you say the hard no, knowing it may cost you a lot? Knowing that God *can* change everything but may not?

These three said it, knowing their lives were on the line, and they never looked back. At least, they didn't look back enough that it was told to us. Who knows what was going on inside their souls, but outwardly they stood there.

And really, isn't that all that matters? They kept standing? They said no and didn't falter? They were brave. They said no. And even when the voices of fear must have been whispering to them, they didn't listen. They stood there in their no and believed that God is still God.

And for it, they were thrown into the furnace.

———

That's the choice they made, the no they said. It was brave, but in the moment when the road split and they could go left or go right, they took the road that said yes to God but no to the easier way.

> Two roads diverged in a yellow wood,
> And sorry I could not travel both
> And be one traveler, long I stood
> And looked down one as far as I could
> To where it bent in the undergrowth;
>
> Then took the other, as just as fair,
> And having perhaps the better claim
> Because it was grassy and wanted wear;
> Though as for that the passing there
> Had worn them really about the same,
>
> And both that morning equally lay
> In leaves no step had trodden black.
> Oh, I kept the first for another day!

Yet knowing how way leads on to way,
I doubted if I should ever come back.

I shall be telling this with a sigh
Somewhere ages and ages hence:
Two roads diverged in a wood, and I —
I took the one less traveled by,
And that has made all the difference.

ROBERT FROST, "THE ROAD NOT TAKEN"

All the difference. *All the difference.*

The road is always going to split. There is always going to be another option or another map altogether. There is always going to be a no that may be expensive but right.

I think about Jeff, the young man I liked for most of my college years. Had I stayed in my college town, where he still lives, I totally think we would have ended up together. But saying yes to Nashville was saying no to Athens, and, as far as I can tell for now, that was a no to Jeff as well.

One of the hardest days of my writing career was ending my relationship with my first agent. He's a good agent, but we weren't working. Too many time zones between us and too many communication issues. I'm a talker. I want to meet and talk and be in the same place and be successful. We were none of those things.

But saying no to continuing our relationship meant what? It meant my career was over. He was the only one who had ever expressed interest in my work, and he was all I knew. To end us was, in many ways, to recognize that my dream of being an author might die along with this partnership. I called him. It was a longer conversation than I expected, but I had to say "No, this isn't working for me" and "No, this isn't going to continue." And we walked away. For ten months I thought this career was gone forever.

A lot of courageous noes make for some beautifully brave yeses. And I guess we never know which ones come first until we are standing at the crossroads, right? It may be easier to determine the yes route, knowing it means saying no. Or maybe it is the no you are sure of, so that tells you where to say yes.

And I'm just not sure you are going to get it right every time — saying the right yes and the right no. I don't get it right all the time. But courage doesn't equal right; courage equals stepping out and trying. Be brave and say yes. But also be brave and say no. Jump on the float. Walk into the furnace. Stand up. Sit down. Get on that flight. Say the thing that courage asks you to say, even if it's the word *no*.

hold on

May 2013
Stumptown Coffee on SW 3rd Ave., Portland, Oregon

            I was calling the cable company to see about changing my plan. Here's the situation: I pay for way more television than I watch. I don't want to cancel cable. I like being able to watch the local news at times (you know, especially during Vanderbilt baseball season), and yet I also would like to keep Food Network because that Pioneer Woman can cook somethin' fierce. Also, Bravo — *The Real Housewives of Atlanta*. Sorry, I'm not sorry.

So I was on the phone trying to figure out if there is a way to have the actual services I want from my cable provider and not pay a gazillion dollars for a hundred channels that just get between me and Kim Zolciak. (Also, *The Real Housewives of Atlanta* star is married to an Atlanta Falcon, which is a goal I have pursued my whole life. So I like her for that too.)

The cable company put me on hold. And there I sat — for twenty-eight minutes.

In those moments, I never know when to hang up. I could be the *very next caller* they speak with, or it could be another half hour. And if I sit here, will they get to me soon, or if I hang up and call back, will I somehow skip over the line of customers on hold and immediately get to speak to a customer care representative? (To which I'd also like to say that they play fast and loose with the idea that they "care" about the "customer." But that's neither here nor there.)

Worst-case scenario? I will sit on hold all day long, waiting to speak to someone, only to realize I have been forgotten.

When do you hang up? For me, it was minute twenty-nine. And I'm still paying more for cable than I want to.

When you come to that crossroad, the moment when you could hold on or let go, what do you do? How do you know what to do?

More than with every other word you've read in this book, I hope you remember this: The road to courage is lit by God's wisdom. His word in the Bible and through the Holy Spirit to you and through others is how you know. You tap into that. You ask for that. You dig into that.

His word is a lamp for your feet (Psalm 119:105). Your feet. Right under you. Look down. Take that step. It's right in front of you.

And when it comes to holding on or letting go, I think you look down and see where the light leads you.

The prophet Isaiah writes, "Whether you turn to the right or to the left, your ears will hear a voice behind you, saying, 'This is the way; walk in it'" (Isaiah 30:21).

It's his still, small voice deep in your knower. It's godly wisdom from a friend. It's a verse or a quote or a moment of clarity when you just know. You will know which way to walk. I promise you will.

———

I say all that to say this. Only you can know the right time in your unique story, but may I push you and encourage you and say, *Please hold on*?

I'm a quitter. It comes way too easy for me to walk away from something that feels hard, whether it's a gymnastics class, a friendship, or a diet. But as I mature and grow up, I'm learning that courage builds when I hang on.

Listen. I've wanted to walk away from this career a lot. And I mean a lot. It gets hard and lonely and frustrating (along with all the good things — don't get me wrong!). But I'm hanging on because I see the light at my feet telling me to keep walking and writing.

Joy Williams has a song called "Golden Thread," and when things seem to be stretching me too thin, I loop that song like nobody's business. Because it reminds me that when I feel like I am just hanging by a thread and it all seems to be unraveling and to simply cut it would be the best bet, that thread may be gold. And it may be worth holding on.

Things can get sticky here. You're in an abusive relationship? I'm not telling you to stay. You're trying to make it out in LA as an actress, and you're literally out of money? I'm not telling you to stay.

Look for the light. The light at your feet. And follow it. And when you know it's right to hold on, hold on. Grip tightly until your hands are sore. But don't let go.

If you're tired of fighting for that prayer that seems to never be answered? Hold on. If you want to walk away from your marriage to a godly man because it has become something different than you thought it'd be? Hold on. (Get counseling, but hold on.) If you have applied to the college of your dreams but haven't heard back yet? Hold on.

Hold on to hope. That's the thing we can't stand to lose. You can let go of jobs or people or hurts, but don't let go of hope.

This book isn't about me being single, but if you think it's been easy to hold on to hope as I've watched my friends pass me in life phases over and over again, oh, friend. Not so much. It's one thing when they get engaged or married. It's another when the babies come. And another when the kids go to school — and I'm still alone at night.

Amy Stroup sings a song called "Hold Onto Hope Love" that has been my companion more nights than I can count as I've cried to God about the rough patches on my hands from holding on so tight to the cliff of hope when it feels like it would be easier to just let go and fall into hopelessness.

And the truth? It would be easier.

But it wouldn't be brave.

It's not the story God is writing with my life. It's not the story God is writing with yours either.

So please. Hold on.

Don't let go because it hurts or because it is hard. Don't let go because you feel like it is ridiculous to hold on. It's not. Hold on.

My friend dreams of adopting, and yet multiple babies come into her family's lives only to go home with the birth mom. But my friend holds on. Christy is tired of running miles and miles every day, but she wants to run a marathon, so she doesn't quit. She holds on. Mike and his wife run a camp for students where the buildings get run-down, the staff turns over, and the pool always smells a little off (just a little). It gets hard to have their jobs. But they see Jesus show up for students every week during the summer, so they hold on. Beth stays home with her four kids under five years of age and sees the dishes pile up and the laundry pile up quicker than she can clean. She has days when she wants to stay in bed or walk away. But she holds on.

> Since God has so generously let us in on what he is doing, we're not about to throw up our hands and walk off the job just because we run into occasional hard times. We refuse to wear masks and play games. We don't maneuver and manipulate behind the scenes. And we don't twist God's Word to suit ourselves. Rather, we keep everything we do and say out in the open, the whole truth on display, so that those who want to can see and judge for themselves in the presence of God . . .
>
> So we're not giving up. How could we! Even though on the outside it often looks like things are falling apart on us, on the inside, where God is making new

life, not a day goes by without his unfolding grace. These hard times are small potatoes compared to the coming good times, the lavish celebration prepared for us. There's far more here than meets the eye. The things we see now are here today, gone tomorrow. But the things we can't see now will last forever.

2 CORINTHIANS 4:1 – 2, 16 – 18 MSG

We just have to hold on. Not a day goes by without God's unfolding grace.

I hate it when people say, "God will never give us more than we can handle," mainly because I don't think it's true and it isn't in the Bible. The Bible says no temptation will come to us that we cannot endure it (1 Corinthians 10:13), but it never says that God has a limit on our swell line and knows not to cross it.

You have to be brave enough to hold on, even when your struggle feels like it's more than your hands can handle.

I want to grab your shoulders, look into your eyes, and say it again. *Hold. On. Don't give up on life. Don't give up on God. Don't give up on yourself.*

Hold on to hope, love.

let go

October 2011
Starbucks in Holy Corner, Edinburgh, Scotland
Seat 61, train ride from Edinburgh to London

I'm a toucher. Not a groper, mind you. I just mean that if I'm sitting beside you or standing around you, I'm probably going to grab your arm, pat your back, or shove you. (The shove usually only happens if I start laughing a lot — and it sometimes looks like a punch. I tend to overexpress. Consider yourself warned.)

Especially when I am leaving. When I am leaving, I want to hold on.

On July 4, 2011, I was exactly one week from moving from Nashville to Edinburgh. The weeks before had been rough, and I mean *rough*. I was terribly sad to leave my community. I knew what God had said about Edinburgh. I wasn't wrong about taking that step. I just was brokenhearted to leave my people. I cried with no warning. Literally. Not even for myself. Every "last" was torturous — including, but not limited to, my last chicken burrito from Baja Burrito. (I'm writing this while in Edinburgh, and my mouth literally just started watering even speaking of Baja. We all have to make sacrifices; mine just looks like chips and roasted tomato salsa.)

So on that sunny day in July, our crew in Nashville had spent the day tubing down the Buffalo River. We laughed as people got flipped out of their tubes by rapids, and we brought enough snacks to float all the way to Florida and never get hungry or thirsty. It began to rain, and we laughed again, as everything we had worked so hard to keep dry in the river below got soaked by the raindrops from above. It was one of those bookmark days, the kind you will tell your kids about.

Exhausted, a little sunburned, and happy, we finished the stretch of river and headed to a fine dinner at Sonic.

Listen, I never claimed we were classy. And you can't judge me for wanting Tater Tots after working all day to keep myself safely in a tube floating down a river. (For those who have never tubed, that sentence was a joke. There is minimal work involved in staying in a tube. But I love any reason I give myself to eat Tater Tots.)

We got back to Nashville just in time to clean up and reconvene for the massive fireworks show that the Fourth of July always guarantees. Apparently a little alone time was all I needed to get my sad emotions going. We met up at Nichole's and walked toward the parking deck, just a friendship amoeba—a blob of people. To my left, Curt—a production manager for a local band and one of the most responsible and kind men in my life. Curt is one of the people on the planet who makes me feel completely safe. To my right, Lyndsay — a fantastic writer and one of my best friends.

As the tears began to puddle right on top of my lower eyelids, I slid my left hand into the bend of Curt's right elbow. We smiled. The tears rolled slowly down my cheeks. If there was a way to stop them, I didn't know it and couldn't have thought through those steps clearly anyway. I said to Lynds, "Hold my hand." And so we walked, the three of us, linked by my sorrow, to see a fireworks show.

I just wanted to feel them. I knew that was what I was giving up by moving away.

Because of modern technology, I don't have to be in the same town to hear and see my friends and family. Thank you, Skype. But I can't feel them. I can't touch them.

I had to sacrifice the presence of my people. I had to let go.

And I feel it happening again here in Edinburgh. I stood by Louise at church on Sunday, and as our friends were baptized in the hot-tub-looking contraption, it was all I could do not to grab her arm. I can't be in the same room with Theo, the one I call my Scottish little brother, without hugging him. I just want to know their presence while I'm here.

Because before I know it, I'll have to let go.

If you could see me now, you would laugh. Maybe. Probably not my mom — she would be sad for me — but the rest of you would be entertained. I'm on a train that departed from Edinburgh Waverley Station, and I'm heading down to London for a week. About ten of my Nashville friends are there, and I'm prepared to do a lot of hugging and hand-holding.

But for now, I'm sitting by the window in seat 61, sharing a table with two businessfolks headed down for meetings. And here I am in my jeans and striped cardigan with The Wedding Band in my ears and tears begging to be released.

I. Am. A. Crier. And just talking about letting go gets my inner waterworks system on alert. But I'm trying to hold it together, mainly for these poor hardworking chaps beside me. (And that's the part that would make my mom sad—the picture of me trying not to cry on a train as it chugs down to London town.)

Letting go has always been hard for me. Yet I have seen, over and over again, that to simply let go is a powerful catalyst God will use to move me toward the next best thing.

I couldn't grab hold of Nashville until I let go of Marietta.

I couldn't grab hold of Edinburgh until I let go of Nashville.

It's always nice, a wee bit easier, to let go when you know what you are grabbing hold of. The monkey bar option, I like to call it. You are willing to let go of the current monkey bar because you can see the next one you want to grab.

(I have to be honest here. I have no arm strength. So monkey bars are about zero percent fun for me. But I do know and understand how they work.)

The deeper call for courage comes when you let go with nothing ahead to grab.

———

It had snowed for days, which is weird for Nashville. Josh texted to make dinner plans, and I cringed. In my mind, I was standing at the end of a plank, and I knew the text was the barrel of the gun in my back. It was time to jump.

It was time to let go.

We had to end. We both knew it. Without a commitment and without a good understanding of what we wanted, we were merely wasting each other's time being *this* invested. *Fish or cut bait*, they say. *Bring on the scissors*, I said.

He was my best friend. His friendship was a place of safety, honesty, and comfort. I loved him. I don't totally know what I mean when I say that. But I know it is how I felt.

And on that December night, heading to a dinner that was meant for us to celebrate the release of my first book, my heart was breaking.

The weather kept everyone in town at home, but not us. We ate our burritos alone in the restaurant and chatted. The windows were fogged, and the room felt stale and almost too warm.

He asked the normal questions that spoke our language, and I answered in a foreign way — short, shallow, lifeless. If he noticed, he didn't say. I tried to do more listening than talking. He was written into every story in my life, and I thought the more I could stay quiet, the more I could write him out.

We finished quicker than usual. We got in his car, and before the doors were closed, I was wiping away the tears from my eyes.

"I'm not dramatic. I'm just emotional. You know that's different, right?" I asked. He nodded.

"What's going on?" I saw in his eyes that he knew, just like I knew. We knew.

I thought of how amputations are always shorter surgeries than the ones where a limb gets repaired. And we began the amputation. A short ten-minute conversation about who we were, who we are, and who we don't think we'll be in the future.

I cried. He didn't. He never does.

We pulled up to my house, and it started to drizzle a cold, almost frozen rain. I looked at him as he stared straight ahead.

"We'll still speak in public, right? I mean, we aren't going to ignore each other, are we? I don't want it to be like that." I spoke with a little shake in my voice, a part of me that only comes out in my mousiest moments.

"Yes. Of course." He half smiled, one of those sad smiles that look more like resignation than mischief.

And when the door to my house closed behind me and I wept out the finale to my roommate, I knew what it felt like to let go.

———

That conversation didn't happen because either Josh or I had a better offer in the hopper. We just let go because we were supposed to let go. Not because something better was in view. God just made it clear that the time had come.

Letting go like that is the hardest. And the days after, when you have to stand by what you know is right — that's when courage has to bubble out of you. It's then that my insides had to be like steel. And all the times that God has been right before, in the Bible and in my life, were on a movie reel through my mind, reminding me of his faithfulness. I watched it, that film on repeat in my head, because I had to know and believe he knows what he is doing (Philippians 1:6).

It may be a relationship or a job or a city or some money or old hurts. When it is time to let go, you know it. Your hands long to ungrip, but your heart begs them to hold on. But only in letting go are your hands free to grab on to the next thing.

Someday I'll look back on that cold night's conversation and know what it was all worth. I'll know why having vacant hands made all the difference.

But for today, I still don't know. Courage doesn't tell you to let go when you know what to grab next. Brave people let go when it's time to let go.

And so I turn these empty hands skyward, trusting they are better off this way.

———

Please let go. Please be brave enough to empty your hands without seeing the next monkey bar.

Sometimes you have to let go of things that are bad for you — addictions, abusive relationships, sinful habits. That takes courage too. It doesn't matter if the thing is good for you or bad for you; if it isn't the *best* for you, you have to let go.

Do you know what I know about you? I know that if

you are meant to let go of something right now, your heart is beating out of your chest. You don't have to ask yourself what it is — that thing is blazing on your insides.

You see the picture of the relationship that isn't right.

You see the dollar sign telling you that giving away that money, letting go of it, is the bravest thing you could ever do.

You see the addiction in its ugly, slimy form.

You see what you're supposed to jump away from even if you don't see what it is you're jumping into.

It brings to mind a favorite verse that, if you are right on the end of that plank, will make you absolutely insane. I'm sorry in advance: "Trust in the LORD with all your heart and lean not on your own understanding; in all your ways submit to him, and he will make your paths straight" (Proverbs 3:5–6).

I let go of Josh because I chose to trust God with all of my heart and not lean into what I understand. I flew away from Nashville to live in a foreign country because I knew that was what submitting to God meant. For all the moments when I have missed courage and chosen the easier path (and my friend, there have been many), I got these two right, and my life will never be the same.

I don't know how, and I can't put the right words to it, but I know the courageous sacrifices are always worth it.

So, friend, let go.

at home

February 2013
Cool Beans, Marietta, Georgia

Bill was the first man I ever loved. He was a tall, blond sixteen-year-old. I was three. He was shy and quiet, but he always talked to me. And he listened because I was then, as I am now, a talker. He loved sitting beside me at dinner. He never missed a family party. He gave me a plastic camera for my third birthday — the flash was a small, multicolored cube on the corner of the camera that turned when you pushed the button. I was sure he was the coolest person who had ever existed on earth.

Bill was my dad's little brother in the Big Brother/Little Brother program through the Boys and Girls Club in our town. I have so many clear memories of Bill. Dad would pick him up and bring him to our house a few times a month, and he would hang out for the day or stay for the weekend. I remember one summer night when he stayed with us. Dad had grilled out, and Bill had just finished showering. It was

133

time to eat, and my mom asked me to holler up the stairs to Bill. He leaned over the banister to say he was almost ready, and I recall being shocked that he didn't have a shirt on. We were a house full of modest girls and a modest dad — *shirts were worn at all times.* (Childhood memories are the weirdest, right?) I met his girlfriend, rode in my dad's car with him, and played cards with him.

I'm telling you, I can still see his face clearly in my mind's eye even thirty years later.

I remember where he was sitting on the couch when I opened that birthday gift, and I can still see his face as he smiled and laughed when I took his picture with my plastic camera with the click-and-turn flash. There was no film in the toy, but he never let on that he knew that.

Dad knew Bill for a long time, having been partnered with him since the kid was eight years old. But for being the first man I ever loved, I did not get enough time with him. Around Christmas in 1983, Bill was killed in a car accident. We returned home from a Christmas family event with my mother's family in Macon, Georgia, and my dad's father was waiting for us in the driveway. I can still see Grandpa Jack through the windshield, standing by his car, waiting to break the news to my dad.

We went in the house, and my mom, sister, and I sat on one couch; my dad sat on the other. Mom pushed us out of her lap and told us to go hug our dad. I felt afraid, but simply because everything felt wrong. I don't know what my dad said to us, but I remember knowing, somehow, even in my little girl head, that Bill was gone forever. This boy I saw as a part of my family would never be in our house again. And my dad was very, very sad.

Dad taught me a lesson with Bill, in his life and in his death, that he has continued to teach me over and over for my entire life: be brave enough to love the people around you, even if it looks like sacrifice and feels like loss.

———

When my sister would talk about going to the mission field internationally, my dad would always say, "People in our own town still need Jesus, you know. Why don't you just stay here?"

Actually, he'd also say, "Why don't you be a missionary to Acworth?" because Acworth is a tiny town about thirty minutes from my parents' house that my father apparently believes is full of heathens.

Dad's funny like that. But actually? He lives that too — the belief that you should be concerned for the people around you. Dad has always made a point to go out of his way to care about the people in our community, whether or not it made him look good.

One of my dad's best childhood friends raised three boys virtually alone. My dad would take the boys out to eat or take us over to hang out with them and play on the playground every so often. Dad has done accounting work for families, even when they couldn't afford the help or weren't able to pay him (though we did get some fresh garden produce a time or two as payment). Dad met with a friend of mine a few weeks ago because she lost her job and didn't know what to do about her lack of income. (Did I mention my dad is supersmart and everyone wants his advice? Well, that.)

Dad serves our local community with his time, money, and advice. It would be easier to just worry about our family. Trust me, we give him plenty to worry about. Instead, he cares for lots of families and does whatever he can to help them. It would be easier to just worry about his own company, but he chooses to care about others and their livelihood.

Marietta, Georgia, is better because Tom Downs lives there.

———

The world needs to hear about Jesus. The world needs to see your courage in action. But you live in your town for a reason.

What is it?

Why are you there?

Why is *here* your spot on the map?

Why have you chosen that town, of all the towns in the world, to be your home?

Maybe you didn't pick it. Maybe it picked you. But you are there. When we think about the puzzle of the person you are, the zip code on your mailing address is an important piece.

———

I've never been moved by a book like I was moved by *Christy* by Catherine Marshall. I first read it as a middle schooler.

In case you haven't read it, please put down this book and immediately pick up *Christy*. (Kidding. Don't.) The book is a fictional retelling of the real life of Catherine Marshall's mother, Leonora Whitaker, who was a schoolteacher in the rural Appalachian mountains of East Tennessee in the early 1900s.

(Trust me, the parallel between Christy Huddleston, my favorite book character ever, and my own life — schoolteachers moving to Tennessee alone without family — is not lost on me. In fact, I probably purposefully find comparisons that aren't as obvious — "Oh, my ..., Christy and I *both* wear dresses and *both* like boys and *both* know how to read. WE ARE THE SAME PERSON." Don't we all do that with our heroes?)

I devoured that book and then started over and did it again. I knew it backward and forward — the characters, the mountain passes, the dramatic twists. I was a superfan. My eighth-grade spring break was spent with my mom and grandmother and best friend touring the filming locations for the *Christy* television show. I have a dream to attend ChristyFest, a yearly convention in Townsend, Tennessee, for fans of the show and book.

Are you getting the theme here? I was (am?) obsessed.

I wanted to know her because I felt like I did, even as a little thirteen-year-old. I dreamed of teaching school before I read *Christy*, but after I read it, I knew beyond any doubt that I wanted to do that for my job. I saw how she served a disadvantaged community in our own country and how education changed the future for each of those students.

It amazed me that she was a missionary in Tennessee.

I didn't know about the Appalachian people and the poverty in that area of the world. As a metro-Atlanta girl, I just could not believe that within driving distance I would come to this same, still struggling community — almost a hundred years after the setting of the book.

My eyes were opened. Growing up in church, I always heard of missionaries in France or Africa or Costa Rica, but I didn't realize the need was so close to us. As a result, I've been on multiple mission trips to the Appalachian area. I read every book I can find on the people group. And when I was deciding where to teach school, I tried to pick locations that served the people of Appalachia.

I met Catherine Marshall's grandson once. He was dating a friend of mine, and they came to church on a Sunday morning. I couldn't get any words out through the tears, which I'm sure he really enjoyed, given that he was an eighteen-year-old kid, but I just couldn't believe I was standing in front of the literal offspring of my hero. I blubbered through some story about how his grandmother's writing and his great-grandmother's life had absolutely changed me, but I don't remember what I said as much as I remember how totally embarrassed I was that I could not even a little bit control my emotions.

And I realized that day that Christy Huddleston was my hero. And my hero never left America. My hero left her family in 1909 and went alone to serve in the hollows of East Tennessee.

Right here. Right in my state. She was brave here.

———

Are you brave enough to find your place even if your place is right here? As a high school senior, I stood in the middle of the town square in Ciudad Cortes, Costa Rica, and shared the gospel with an interpreter, and yet one of my best friends from high school was not a believer and I didn't even talk to him about Jesus.

Why does it sometimes take more courage at home? Why am I more willing to sign up for a mission trip to Mexico than to serve the homeless in downtown Nashville?

Being brave at home means serving.

When my small group of college students recently celebrated our one-year anniversary, we decided to serve. Well, that's not totally true. The girls knew we were doing something special, and since we eat dinner together every Tuesday, they may have thought there would be a special meal or a special guest. Instead, I bamboozled them and only served peanut butter and jelly sandwiches and fruit, and we loaded into two cars and headed downtown. They didn't know what we were doing, but at this point, after a year together, they trust me enough to know I'm not kidnapping them and yet to never be surprised when I have a cockamamie plan.

We arrived in downtown Nashville and made our way to a large overpass, where many people were gathered under the bridge. A praise and worship band was playing, using one of those sound systems that kinda hurts my ears — like a traveling preacher from the 1980s would use. Homeless people sat in rows and rows of chairs, each with a plate of food on their lap as volunteers wove in and out and helped everyone get settled.

It happens every Tuesday night in our town. The Bridge's outreach ministry feeds homeless men, women, and children a huge and healthy meal, and then someone shares the gospel. As the people leave, they are able to fill bags with fresh produce donated by local grocery stores.

My small group and I had never gone before, but our church goes once a month on Tuesday nights so we knew it was a respected ministry to be involved with.

The girls were nervous and hovered close to me like chicks to a hen for the first few minutes. But then they just got in line with the other volunteers and started to serve. Carrying food. Helping others find a seat. Passing out fruits, veggies, or huge bags of bread at the end of the night. We were there for a few hours, but the experience stuck with all of us much longer.

It takes courage to serve in new places just down the street from your normal places. I was so proud of my girls — jumping right in and being part of an experience they didn't know was going to happen.

———

I didn't have a place to live when I moved back to Nashville from Scotland. All my belongings were in a storage unit somewhere in West Nashville, and I no longer had an address. It was Thanksgiving, and I planned to find something around Christmas.

Before leaving Nashville the previous summer, I had joked with Luke and Heather about moving in with them when I got back. Sometime in the fall, Luke skyped me and said the joke was an actual offer. I was welcome to stay with them for a couple of weeks while trying to find a place.

I interrupted their life. I added an entire human to their two-human household. I needed a key and a bed and a bathroom and the internet.

Coming home from being overseas for six months, I was worried about reverse culture shock. It's a real thing, y'all. Being surrounded by a foreign culture, attempting to make it your own, and then coming back home — it can cause a normally sane person to lose it a little bit.

And I'm not normally sane. So. You've gotta factor that in too.

But living with Luke and Heather was the most comfortable, warmest, friendliest environment. We decorated the Christmas tree, went to see movies in sweats, and walked to dinner at Edley's, the new barbecue restaurant in the neighborhood. In fact, another friend, Adam, lived with us as well, so we just became a little family of four for that holiday season.

I think their sacrifice rescued me from the pain of readjusting to Nashville and America. I truly do.

New Year's Day came, and I still hadn't found a place to live. Weeks had accidentally turned to months, and it wasn't until mid-February that I was packing my things and moving to a house just down the street.

Luke and Heather never complained. We talked about it openly and honestly multiple times, but they just kept giving — their space, their time, their money, their hearts.

It's brave to let a person live in your house who isn't your family.

It's brave to serve the less fortunate in your own zip code.

It's brave to give your life and your comfort so that others can have life.

It's brave to teach your family the importance of investing in your own community.

The longer I live, the more I think I'm figuring out that courage often looks like sacrifice and service. In the places where you find the most comfort, you have to have a little extra something to give there. Home is where we rest. Home is where we find peace, so to give from there, to sacrifice in that place, is to sacrifice deeply, I think. It's brave.

around the world

June 2013
Lipscomb University Starbucks, Nashville, Tennessee

I don't really do yard work. When I was growing up, and this is 100 percent true, my grandmother did all the yard work for our family. She loved to ride that lawn mower wherever tall grass would take her. It is one of my favorite memories — seeing her ride around our three acres in polyester pants and a massive floppy hat.

But last week, even with my lack of training, it was high time to take on the vines, weeds, and shrubs that had taken over the front of my home. On the brightest days of summer, these two shrubs were so overgrown that barely any light came in through the windows. It was a mass of mess. Through the center of both bushes, which were both taller than me and wider than I could wrap my arms around, shot up some sort of thick-trunked leafy weed. So picture massively overgrown greenery with a seven-foot weed shooting skyward from the middle. I asked a landscaper friend of mine what kind of weed

143

he thought it was. His response when he saw it? "Annie, those are maple trees growing up through your shrubs."

Oh.

So. You've got the idea of what I was working with.

I don't own any yard equipment per se, so I went to Matt and Amber and borrowed hedge trimmers, thick clippers, and a pair of gloves. Fully decked out and with my iPod blasting some tunes, I went after those two rogue shrubs, and their maple tree invaders, with a vengeance.

I pulled vines that took me twenty feet across my yard before they reached their end. I trimmed and hedged and chopped and clipped and carried ten armloads of weeds and all other manner of leafy strands to the trimmings pile in the backyard.

It took me two solid hours to get these two plants to look like anything manageable.

There was a remaining section of tangled mess on the right shrub that I grabbed with an "I am almost done with this" superstrength and pulled as hard as I could. The overgrowth came unattached from the shrub itself and ripped as I stepped backward until I froze.

When I heard baby birds chirping.

(This is the part of the story when you are going to realize that at times I am a monster. Not on purpose, but a monster nonetheless.)

Yep, I had just torn apart a nest full of baby birds. That's when I realized that from the tree behind me, the mama bird had been *losing her mind* for the last twenty minutes as I got closer and closer to her babies, and her sound was just registering with me.

I stopped immediately and looked down into the nest. Somewhere in the recesses of my mind, I remembered a teacher telling me never to touch baby birds or their mama will abandon them for eternity, or something like that, so I didn't touch them. But I released the vines and rubbish to dangle from the bush, the birds and nest tightly tangled in the middle.

I stepped back cautiously, surprisingly frightened of that mama bird wailing behind me. I found this to be just the right time to silently tiptoe backward to my front porch and take a seat and drink some water.

I watched that nest closely. The mama did fly over and stand on the top of the shrub, and as she chirped out instructions, her little baby birds wiggled and squished out of the nest between vines and limbs and hopped from shrub to ground. They flapped their little wings, all three of them alive (I thought for sure I was a birdie murderer, so I was really grateful for that), and traveled off together to what I am going to always tell myself was a very happy and productive future.

There is nothing scarier than leaving the nest, I would bet. Especially when the exit is prefaced by a violent shaking and ripping apart of your home. (Ahem. My apologies for that part, birdies.) But it was interesting to watch them regain their footing and adjust to their new location before hopping out.

And that's exactly what they did.

———

I have friends who live in China. Turkey. Prague. Asia. The Middle East. Costa Rica. India. Scotland. Ghana. Brazil.

South Africa. Italy. All of them are Americans who are long-term missionaries to foreign cultures.

I'm not a collector of missionary friends. International missions is just a core value that my church instilled in all of us as we grew up. I can remember being at our church's summer camp as a fifth grader and learning every day about a different area of the world where the people there needed to hear about Jesus.

(This is also the year of camp when I learned how to sing two songs that helped me memorize the books of the Bible. I'll sing them for you anytime. You're welcome.)

As I continued from elementary age into youth group, we had many opportunities to travel out of the country on mission trips. I went to France, Costa Rica, Mexico, and Africa. We had to raise our own funds and attend weekly meetings, but our adult leaders were brave enough to pack up sometimes upward of sixty high schoolers and take them across oceans or borders.

Now, as an adult, I am certain they were insane.

Some of my fondest memories from my teen years come from those mission trips — riding bikes on the cobblestones of the Palace of Versailles, learning traditional dances in the church building of Ciudad Cortes, Costa Rica, after a long day of building and sweating. Our church provided opportunities to see the world that I might not have otherwise had.

More importantly, I saw God.

When Costa Rican children gathered around us during bilingual VBS and made bracelets that share the gospel to take home to their families, I saw God.

When Parisian church buildings, usually empty, became filled to capacity to see a bunch of American high schoolers do a variety show, I saw God.

When we met hundreds of Scottish students at a university student fair just outside of Edinburgh, I saw God.

———

The map can take you anywhere. Absolutely anywhere. My friend Shireen moved to Africa to teach school right after college. We mailed letters back and forth, and I remember thinking she was living the kind of life people write books about. She gave her time to educate people in other parts of the world and share Jesus while she was at it.

I know people who have lived outside of their country for months, others for years, and still others for decades. Not everyone is Amy Carmichael, a missionary to India in the early 1900s who didn't go on furlough for fifty-five years. I personally maxed out at five months and twenty-eight days. Being brave doesn't have a predetermined length of time that says success. My bravest moment when I decided to move to Scotland wasn't the last day; it was the first. I could have gone home after a week and still would have known that I had done the brave thing.

Tammy is a missionary in India. She's been there for fifteen years. When she arrived, she had eighty dollars in her pocket and a few connections for doing ministry. Now, many years and many miracles later, Tammy has forty-eight children in her care and a staff of ten, and God shows up for them all the time.

She's not brave because of the length of time she's been

there or the amount of children she and her staff care for (though both of those things are amazing). She is brave because she went. Because she decided to forgo her life here in America for a life she didn't know.

This isn't to say that America is the best place to live and if you live anywhere else you are sacrificing. Nope, I don't think that's the case. Courage isn't leaving America for another part of the world; courage is leaving home. Leaving the culture you know for one you don't know. Because every day in that new place will provide opportunities for you to come face-to-face with something you don't know, and yet somehow to choose joy. Because you chose to be there. Because you chose to be brave.

———

I got injured in Scotland. It's a bizarre story really, but not too shocking for the people who know me. I pay for health insurance not because I get sick but because I get hurt. A lot. I'm clumsy. My mind moves better than my body, and I'm far too distracted, usually talking, when I should be focused on walking. Also, at times I have managed to forget that just because I could once do an activity—say, a cartwheel when I was ten years old—doesn't necessarily mean I can do it now at thirty-three.

But on this late summer day in Scotland, when I had only lived there for a month or so, I was merely getting up from the couch and walking to put a DVD in the player when somehow I managed to get my legs tangled in my computer cord. It was almost like some tiny troll had come and tied the cords around my ankles so that when I stood up, I couldn't take a step. I tripped and slammed the front of my left shin into the corner of the coffee table and knew immediately it was bad.

Not to be dramatic (clearly, I'm *never* that), but I thought I might have broken my leg. I knew for certain it was a deep cut because it did that white thing right before it started bleeding out. And I'm talking b l e e d i n g o u t.

I skyped my mother immediately and tried to show her, but it came across looking grainy and wouldn't stop bleeding so she could assess the damage. I was totally panicked.

In Nashville, I would have known to go to the ER and what to take. As a matter of fact, a few years before when I had fallen off my porch on 11th Avenue South in Nashville and tore all the ligaments in my left ankle, that's exactly what I did. But in Edinburgh? I didn't know the first thing to do.

To cut (ouch) to the chase, I didn't do anything for a few days but just tried to control the bleeding (*that didn't stop for nine hours, y'all*). Finally, I went to the pharmacy down in the Bruntsfield neighborhood drugstore, where the Asian-Scottish pharmacist informed me I had made a huge mistake by not going that first day to the A&E (I didn't even know what that was but learned it stood for Accident & Emergency) and that I was going to have a massive scar (I do). It looks like a fat, brown caterpillar right smack on the middle of my very pale shin. It's ugly, but I guess it was cheaper than getting an "I will always remember living in Edinburgh" tattoo.

Going into the world means giving up your neighborhood ER to learn about an A&E. It means not having access to some of your favorite things or people or places in order to make somewhere else your place and make new friends your people. It means you may eat something weird every day, or, as in my case in Scotland, it may be close to what you are used to but just a bit off — and that can be infuriating when you are homesick.

I don't care if you are there for six days or six months, when you go into the world, you are trading your life for a foreign life. And that takes courage. That's a new map, a map that may have a language you don't know or street names you can't decipher or cars on the wrong side of the road.

If you've never gone, go. If you've never had a moment when no one around you speaks your language or shares your pigment or knows how elementary school works, you need to go. You *need* that. You need to see that the world is big and diverse and maybe God doesn't look or sound the way you always thought he did because the world has a lot of different-looking and different-sounding people, all who are made in his image.

Save up your money. Raise your money. Connect with a mission-sending organization or a nonprofit organization. Be brave enough to send that first email that says, "Can I go to Africa with y'all?" or "Yes, I'd like to be on that mission team to Mexico."

Do whatever it takes to expand your map. Because if you will go where you've never gone before, you will see God like you've never seen him before.

every day you have

March 2013
The Well Coffeehouse, Nashville, Tennessee

I miss my grandmother, Ruth. I grew up with her acting like my second mother, as she and my grandfather lived across the driveway from us. I saw them every day. I thought my grandmother was sweet, and I knew she loved me way more than I deserved. She was gutsy and funny and always wanted to walk on the beach when we were vacationing and absolutely loved to hang out with me and my sisters. She was educated and employed. She was a great cook and a voracious reader. She also saw more than her fair share of heartbreak and troubles.

And man, was she determined. She would tell us stories of her meager upbringing in the cotton fields of middle Georgia — how she would work in the fields with her siblings and how their family canned vegetables from the garden. Her first husband left her — literally just left one day — and so she became a single divorced woman in the

1940s. Her subsequent marriage to my grandfather, a widower, caused much clacking around town and left her an outcast. Ma, as we called her, was a librarian at the local high school, Sprayberry High School, and she taught us how to care for books that were not our own.

During my first summer after starting college, my mother, grandmother, great-aunt, and I went on a trip to Savannah, Georgia. We stayed in a bed-and-breakfast and toured around the town. One night, as we were sitting in the library area with other people staying at the bed-and-breakfast, a gentleman from the northern part of the United States asked me about school. I explained that I had just finished my first year at the University of Georgia. He said, "Oh, are you the first educated member of the family?"

My naive self thought he meant the first of the girls in my nuclear family, so I said yes, being that I am the oldest sister.

Ma quickly, and with passion, said, "No sir, she is not. I have my master's degree from the University of Georgia, and her mother has a law degree." Apparently he thought we were country folk who had just learned to read and that I was the first to ever attend a higher education facility — and my grandmother would not stand for that.

She loved us and God just as fiercely as she defended her education and family. I knew my grandmother for twenty-nine years, and as best as I can remember, she was always studying the Bible or praying. She kept lists on a notepad of everyone she was praying for. She sent me letters when I was at camp and at college, letting me know she was praying for me and what she was praying about. She took intense Bible study classes that required a lot of study and effort. And she loved it.

In 2001, while I was on a mission trip to Kentucky, my grandmother had a stroke. She lived, though never the same again, for eight more years. As I watched her for those years, she always felt like a survivor to me. As I heard more stories of what her life was like from her and my grandfather and her siblings and my mom, I began to see a fuller portrait of the kind of woman she was, the things she went through, the sacrifices she made. So it surprised me when she died. I guess I thought she was too strong to die.

She would say in her last days that God kept her on earth to pray for us — her children and grandchildren. That she felt her purpose on this planet was to cover us, intercede for us, and ask God to direct us. That's brave to me.

————

I don't think you have to be in the prime of your life to be brave. Though a recent college graduate has definite advantages over a mom or grandmother or high schooler when it comes to "I want to pack up my life and do something crazy," I don't think courage is limited like that.

Ma was courageous in choosing to live when her body didn't have much life to offer, and she was eighty-nine years old before she took her last breath.

And I see twentysomethings stepping into jobs and opportunities that aren't easy and require bravery.

As a kid, one of my favorite things to listen to was G.T. and the Halo Express. Each tape featured a story of kids visited by angels, and those angels, led by G.T., would help the children solve life issues. (I'm sure this in no way led me to constantly think I saw angels as a child.) During the cassette capers, the children in the stories would learn Bible verses in song form. This has come in quite handy for me as an adult because I can still recite Scriptures and sing them to those very tunes. And I think of the song for Deuteronomy 7:9. I'll sing it for you.

> *Know therefore that the Lord your God is God.*
> *He is the faithful God, keeping his covenant of love,*
> *Keeping his covenant of love to a thousand generations,*
> *To a thousand generations of those who love him and keep*
>   *his commands.*

Fictional angels taught me that song, but the Scripture is true. It doesn't matter what your age is, if you love God and keep his commands, you are starting something for a thousand generations. And probably you are on the receiving end of that as well. I know I certainly am because of Ma and others who came before her.

Because my first few books were written to teen girls, I get lots of emails from teen girls. As you can imagine. Bless them. And so many of their letters amaze me — the things they are willing to do and say for the sake of the gospel. One girl told me she talked about Jesus openly for the first time at her lunch table, and then two girls asked her about Jesus later.

I don't know how long ago you were in high school, but surely you can remember the kind of courage that takes. The risk. The potential social implications. It's all still real and, dare I say, worse for students today.

I think it is brave to join a sorority at a major university and desire to live a life that honors God.

I think it is brave to be an elementary school student and tell your friend that you are praying for his sick dad.

I think it is brave to graduate from college and take a job in a big city where you don't know anyone.

I think it is brave to be a mom.

I think it is brave to move to China and smuggle Bibles to the underground church.

I think it is brave to return to work after years away.

I think it is brave to give up your child for adoption because you realize that raising a kid as a single sixteen-year-old mother isn't the best life he could have.

I don't know how old you are. But I know the lie you hear. You are too young. You are too old. You don't know enough, or you know too much. The truth is that courage doesn't have an expiration date. Courage doesn't have a marker that says, "You must be taller than THIS to ride this ride."

You were meant to be brave. Your map is yours from day one. Of course, a fifth grader isn't going to be ready to move alone to Africa, but she may be ready for a mission trip. God plants dreams in our hearts early. He hands us talents far before we know exactly how to use them. And the young ones? They aren't afraid to think about those talents, to push into whatever that dream is, to be brave naturally.

I have friends who are sure that life has passed them by—that their opportunity to be brave has come and gone. That is sadder to me than anything—you are not too old! My grandmother was brave until her final breath at the age of eighty-nine. And my mom is like her. Not too many years ago, my mom had to stand up for truth in front of a crowd of people who mattered greatly to her but disagreed with her. Some were older — friends of my grandparents — and many were her peers. It was very painful to watch her go through it, but it was impactful on me. She stood up for truth and righteousness when people she loved and respected wouldn't.

And her daughters saw it all.

Remember. Courage is for every age.

everything you have

November 2012
Portland Brew (the dark side), Nashville, Tennessee

It is Saturday morning. (Not like *early*, mind you — I'm not the early morning pensive writer type.) I'm sitting alone on a rainy morning in my favorite coffee shop. It's quiet today, though really, it's quiet here every day. Somehow, Portland Brew has gotten the reputation that if you are gonna sit here, you need to whisper. Virtually a public office space shared by many throughout the day, it's a place you come to work. So this is pretty much the silent library of the coffee shop scene in Nashville.

But today it is especially quiet.

There are two sides in this coffee shop (where, ironically, I only drink chai tea) — the light side, where the wooden tables reflect the sunshine that pours in from the wall of windows, and the dark side. On the dark side, where I sit today, there is little sunlight, especially on this drizzly morning. I'm the only one on this side today, except for the random passerby headed to the bathrooms.

It's probably better this way.

I'm glad I'm by myself today. Writing this is something I have to do alone. My boots are propped up in the seat across from me, and before I even began, I closed my eyes, gently placed my fingers on the keyboard, and did some slow-breathing exercises.

Then I began to type.

And here I am, three-ish paragraphs in, and my heart is already in my throat and tears are welling up in my eyes.

This chapter is going to break my heart. And heal it.

———

When I started writing professionally, I made a decision: I was not going to write about being single.

Those people who write about being single are annoying. That is a vast generalization, I know. But in general, I find that books for single Christians fall into one of two categories — superhappy or supermad. The superhappy author makes me feel guilty for the days when I don't feel happy about being single. The supermad author makes me roll my eyes because I think, "Seriously? You complained for 160 pages? I bet you are a pleasure to be friends with."

I never wrote about singleness because I hate being annoying. It's one of the things I avoid most.

But on a deeper level, I didn't want to write about something that was so. stinking. personal. Because when you desire to be married, pray and believe that God hears you, and then buzz by your thirty-third birthday still single, that junk is personal.

It's not just about being alone at the dinner table or in the bed; it's about unanswered prayers and how to face a God who can do something about those unanswered prayers but doesn't. I didn't want to write about that. It gets deep and intimate and all up in my business.

So I avoided it. For years.

Until I lived in Scotland.

I can't remember the date, but I remember the day. Summer had barely turned into autumn. My freshly washed clothes were drying on the foldable rack beside my one window overlooking the Merchiston campus of Edinburgh Napier University. The window was cracked. It was almost too cold, but the difference in drying time of the clothes, especially jeans (have mercy, they take forever to air dry!), made it absolutely worth it.

I wasn't having a quiet time or anything. Not praying or reading the Bible or doing anything particularly spiritual. I don't remember doing anything particular at all. I sat on my bed in the midmorning, and I heard a whisper in my heart — "It's time to write about being single."

I knew that voice. He's been speaking to my heart for years. And the voice of the One who knows me and loves me gets easier to recognize as I grow older.

I dropped my head and closed my eyes. Where was this map taking me? I trust that God has given me one, and I'm trying to follow it, but I just couldn't understand the path beneath my feet. I didn't feel defeated. I just know a moment of surrender when it is on me. The invisible white flag was in my hands, the flag that said I didn't have to talk about my most personal things, and without my full permission, that flag was raising. I had surrendered before I even gave myself any other option. It was like I was being given a choice, but not really given a choice. Do you know that feeling? You know the right thing to do, you don't want to do it, but you wouldn't dare do anything else?

Yeah. Me too.

I can't be silently single anymore.

———

I am living a life I never planned. And it has required more courage than I ever thought could fit in this five-foot-six-inch frame. I am, honestly, shocked that I am thirty-three and have no husband and no children. But there is this thing in me, deep down in my knower, that is a fireball of hope. Not necessarily hope in the "I am *for sure* getting married someday" way, but hope in the "God knows what he is doing" kind of way.

Hold on to hope, love.

I thought it would be way cooler to write about this later in my life. Like, when I am married to some awesome dude and we have three kids and a nice kitchen and I drive a cool mom SUV and tiny shoes are scattered all throughout our house. Then I could tell all the Christian singles to "hang in there because God has an amazing plan for your life!!" And the section on singleness would be full of exclamation points because I find exclamation points to be very! encouraging! and uplifting!

But I am not going to wait. I think there is something

really powerful about being smack in the middle of the unwanted season and being able to look you right in the eyeball (which I would if I could) and say,

You are going to survive this, friend.

God has not forgotten you.

Your life and your desires are important to God.

It's not my job to be the poster child for Single Christian Girls. Please don't expect that of me or these words on the page. I am not perfect. I don't handle relationships perfectly. I don't know everything there is to know about how to manage this season — friendships with men, sex, boundaries, roles, career pursuits, all that stuff. I am not here to claim ultimate wisdom on how to do this.

I just want to tell you, from one in the trenches of this season of singleness, that I am going to make it just fine. And if you are single and want to be married, you are too.

God hears us when we pray.

God knows our hearts better than we do.

You are allowed to feel like this season requires courage from you to get out of bed, to stay out of his or her bed (whoever he or she is), to move to a new city or a new church or any of that — and to do it alone.

There are hard days in this and there are easy days. But there are never days when you have been abandoned.

And it's good that we talk about it. Because you need to hear the truth of the gospel of love — the one that says we are never alone or abandoned or forgotten. And I need to hear it too. We need to talk openly, bravely, and often.

So I have. And I am. And I will.

I promise.

My dad texted me this morning with that simple, family inside joke — "Who loves ya? Dada. Dada" — that is mainly just meant to remind me that he loves me. He didn't know this section of *Let's All Be Brave* was born today. He didn't know I needed his long-distance support in these writing hours. But I am grateful.

We can talk about the parts of singleness that are really fun — there are so many — and the parts that are heartbreaking, and everything in between. I'm here not to be an expert but just a friend, to tell you my stories like we were sitting together (at a louder coffee shop) and to figure out how to maneuver this season. With grace. With hope. With joy. With honesty.

With courage.

I still feel the pull to be silently single. It would be easier. I wouldn't have to tell some of the embarrassing/sad personal stories you've read throughout this book, many of them happening in the singleness that I wear every day, and I would just get to hunker down with my best friends, on the good days and the bad, and float down this river tied to the ones who know me well. But as much as I willingly surrendered to the voice of God on that day in Edinburgh, Scotland, I know this is going to hurt sometimes. And I am not strong enough to write about this.

But I'm still typing, so I guess we're doing something right. The truth is, I am doing this with no strength of my own. Trust me. The inner Annie is screaming and pushing away from this keyboard like it is a poisonous snake.

everything you have

It's God in me, gently asking me if I'm willing to be brave for you like I'm asking you to be brave for others.

If it is my time to talk about being single, then it is the time that will bring God the most glory and us the most good. We all have these things, whether or not your thing is singleness. We walk through seasons that are filled with unmet expectations and potential for radical hope. Career path changes. Fertility struggles. Illness. And it would be easy to hold quietly to those insecurities, to feign to the world that you are okay, you are in control, you have the power here.

But me? I am not the powerful one. I'm just the broken one who has found a treasure I know I need to share.

———

A woman has just come to the dark side of Portland Brew. She is slight with stringy blonde hair to her shoulders. She is reading some thick book — at first I thought it was the Bible, but at second glance, it isn't. And she is crying. Not weeping, just tears dripping down, and every now and again, she sniffles.

Isn't that funny. Two women in the same coffee shop. Just one table apart. (I will never know why, in an empty room, she picked the table next to me.) She reads, and she cries. I write, and the tears can't be contained either.

We are on the same journey, she and I, at two different ends of a pile of written words. Her, experiencing the end, the finished product; me, the beginning, the words landing on the page for the first time.

I am moved by her, the other woman on the dark side. By her ability to honestly respond to the words on the pages as she reads. I pray that for you today, even as her sniffles continue, that as you read this, you will respond honestly. Hug this book close to your chest or launch it with force across the room. I don't know what the honest response looks like for you. But I know in the deepest places that you want to be courageous with everything you have. And today? This is what you have. To be brave here is to know that, no matter what your marital status is, male or female, always single or happily married, or every spot in between, you are never alone.

———

I sat at dinner last week with two of my friends from college and their parents. There were eight of us, sweet families that have known me through many UGA football seasons. (That's how we judge long spans of time in Athens, Georgia.) Because I hadn't seen them for a year or so, it felt like we had a lot of catching up to do.

One of the moms asked me about my time in Scotland—where I went, what I did. (You already know everything I told her. Don't worry.) She asked caring questions, the kind that only someone who loves you can ask.

And then she said, "Wow, I can't believe you did that all by yourself. I don't think I could have done that."

I almost laughed right then and there, staring at her face. I wanted to say back, "So exactly what other choice did I have, ma'am?" But instead I just smiled—because I know about me what you know about me.

I can't believe I did that all by myself either.
But I'm so glad I did.

———

As I told you, I wanted to be a missionary to Scotland for eleven years. *Eleven years.* Multiple times in my twenties, I had the opportunity to move there for a season or two.

A mission training school.

A youth group internship.

A children's ministry position.

I always said no. Every time.

The timing wasn't ever quite right, I never felt like it was God's best plan, but also, in the back of my head . . .

I was scared.

I was scared that moving to Scotland would mean I would never get married.

So I never did. I let an entire decade go by in hopes that choosing America meant choosing marriage. Now, I'm not saying that staying in America was out of God's will. I know he did good things with my life in that decade; I just know that each time one of those opportunities was placed before me, the fear whispered to me. And I listened.

When I turned thirty, I sat with a few friends in rocking chairs on a front porch. I was talking about how much I expected of this next decade.

And I said, "I'm moving to Scotland."

The new opportunity with Crossroads Church came about. (Four times is the charm? Apparently.) And I knew this was my chance. The right chance. The right opportunity to say yes to God and no to the fear.

I said no in my twenties. I let the fear of being alone, the fear of singleness, keep me from things. And I wasn't going to do that in my thirties.

"What if I look back in ten years," I said to my friend Mary Katherine, "and I'm still single *and* I've said no for another decade, waiting for something that still hasn't come?"

That became my biggest fear—waiting for a marriage I'm not guaranteed, keeping me from doing good things that bring glory to God *right now*.

So I moved to Scotland, and you know what? My life is *so* much richer because of my experience living on the other side of the pond. Saying yes to that open door, ignoring the fear, has made me a better human and someday, hopefully, a better wife.

———

I want to say it again. Being single does not mean you are alone. You never are. I've heard this is true, though I have yet to prove it, but marriage doesn't solve your alone feelings.

Courage doesn't have a list when it comes to singleness. I'm not going to tell you you're supposed to move out of the country or you're supposed to sign up on an online dating site (though I think if you haven't tried it, you totally should). I'm not going to give you a checklist that, if you can tick every box, will prove, once and for all, that you are a brave singlet.

I'm just going to say again what I find to be the truest.

Be brave enough to believe you are never alone. Say yes to dates, mission trips, volunteer opportunities, weekends at the beach — knowing that whether you fly alone or bike alone or lie alone in your bed, Jesus is near. You are never alone, my friend. Never.

And really, the thing that keeps us from the brave thing? Fear that we're in this by ourselves. We. Aren't.

In Matthew 28:20, Jesus says one sentence that slays that fear: "And surely I am with you always ..." *Surely he is.*

My Bible quietly falls open to a tear-crinkled page of the Old Testament as I sit here, and just like an old song on the radio calls out moments in the recesses of your mind, seeing these words in Isaiah brings back memories long forgotten of days when my singleness made me feel completely abandoned and forgotten.

The day before I turned twenty-nine, I couldn't get out of bed. I have never been that sad before. But on that day, July 6, 2009, I was absolutely, unequivocally heartbroken. I rolled over, grabbed my computer from the floor, and wept as I emailed my lifelong friends Haley and Molly.

I don't remember the whole email, and to be honest, I'm not going to search through my archives. I don't want to read it again. But I remember one very dramatic line: "I can't do this another day."

You want me to get ugly honest about what it can be like to be a single Christian woman when you don't want to be single?

Sometimes you don't think you can do another day.

And that's fair and that despair is real and that hurt

is legit. But then, those words from Isaiah reach from the page to grab my face and pull me close, to say straight to my eyes and my heart, "YOU ARE NOT ALONE."

> So do not fear, for I am with you;
> do not be dismayed, for I am your God.
> I will strengthen you and help you;
> I will uphold you with my righteous right hand.
>
> ISAIAH 41:10

The Message talks straight into my bones — know what I mean?

> Don't panic. I'm with you.
> There's no need to fear for I'm your God.
> I'll give you strength. I'll help you.
> I'll hold you steady, keep a firm grip on you.

He has a firm grip on you, friend.
You are not alone.

the why

I got to travel to Honolulu, Hawaii, to
speak at a conference. (I know, sacrificing for the gospel.)
One afternoon before the conference started, I left the
Thurstons' home on Spiffy Lane and went into town for
some writing time. I walked into the Kailua Starbucks to
write for a bit and looked around to see zero tables available. I didn't really have a plan B for where to write, so I
went ahead and got in line for my drink.

A table opened up between a vacationing couple and
three tan and adorable surfer dudes. The surfers were
talking about their marriages, so I tuned out because, ya
know, they have wives already.

I began to unpack, and just because of proximity (the
tables were *close*, y'all), I couldn't help but check back into
their conversation — and I heard them talking about loving
their wives like Christ loves the church. They talked about

absolute truth and how God is the only thing that is absolute, and suddenly I realized I was watching two of them share Jesus with the third.

My heart began to race. My brain was praying for them before I even realized it. They were saying the hard things to this guy—that he needed Jesus, that there is no other way but Jesus, that if he wanted to know Jesus personally, it could happen right here and right now.

You know why we have to be brave? Because courage changes lives. And eternity.

I know, you think I'm being dramatic maybe, but listen. That guy? Sitting to my right, hearing how Jesus is the answer? His life is forever different, his future is forever altered, because those two surfers were brave enough to say the thing.

My drink wasn't ready, but I stood up anyway. I can't explain it, but I liken it to the fact that at the end of a University of Georgia football game, when things are on the line, I like to pace. I felt that same thing in me as I heard these twentysomething guys talking about Jesus.

As I was about to walk from my table to the drink counter, a couple at another table stopped me. The husband, probably in his mid-fifties, said, "That's a nice laptop." To be fair, I have a very basic computer, so this was the weirdest lead-in sentence I'd heard in a while.

"Thanks," I responded. "I'm an author so, you know, I gotta take the office with me."

(Please insert an awkward laugh here from me because, well, I did.)

He asked what I wrote. "Memoir-type nonfiction books

for Christians," I told him — and he said, "WOW, WE ARE CHRISTIANS TOO!" in as excited a voice as you just imagined. Then he placed his hand on my shoulder and asked if he could pray for me.

Brave. Brave. Brave.

What kind of Starbucks was that place? What are they putting in the drinks that made all these people do the scary thing?

I don't know. But yes, I let him pray for me. I never turn that stuff down. I don't remember all the words he prayed, but I will never forget that he asked. It changed me.

Seeing other people be brave makes you want to be brave too.

That's why you'll see rational adults going down a loopty-loop waterslide even if they don't want to, because they want to show the kids it isn't scary.

It's a domino effect.

That's why we have to start. It's why we have to go first. It's why we have to be brave — so that others will be inspired to be brave as well.

As we've discussed, other people can stand with you, encourage your courage, and cheer for you. But the real joy is when we get to be the ones who lead others to a new level of bravery. Sure, I could insert a quote from William Wallace here, but you know how I feel about Scotland, so that would be totally predictable.

"They may take our lives, but they will never take ..."

Seriously. I won't.

"... our freedom!"

Sorry. I did.

171

I saw a picture in my head one time as a friend told me a story of his trip through the jungle.* He could see the path at his feet before him, but if he looked straight ahead, the brush was so thick he couldn't see anything but the vines and leaves tangled at eye level.

He was leading a team, and so it was up to him to use his machete (don't you know he *loved* telling me this part of the story) to chop at the overgrowth to make a way for his people to head down the path. He got scraped up a good bit, but, as he tells it, that was just a minor setback in the bigger story where he was the hero — yes, he called himself a hero — the story that there was a way to walk and it was up to him to make sure those behind him had clear access to travel.

A few years later, far, far away from the jungles of Brazil, I sat across the table in a coffee shop here in Nashville as a young single girl told me of her aches and pains and the faith issues that, in her mind, were directly related to her singleness. (I. Hear. Ya. Sister.) She didn't cry, but I held a napkin in my grip because I thought for sure she would at any moment. She told me stories — many that I felt she was pulling from my own journal as a twentysomething single Christian gal — and I told her what I never knew to tell myself.

I know.

*This section is based on a July 21, 2012, post titled "Trailblazer," which originally appeared on the (in)courage blog, an online home for the hearts of women (www.incourage.me/).

It hurts.

But God has not forgotten you.

He is showing you his love for you, even now.

Believe him. Believe his Word. Believe his heart.

The year 2011 is when I started writing publicly about my single life. She had noticed. And she asked me, "Why now? What is it about your thirty-first year that made you finally want to talk about it?"

"God." I said. "He just made it clear this was the right time."

Without hesitation, she said, "I'm so glad. We all need trailblazers. Now that I see that *you've* done this, I genuinely think I can do it too."

I almost laughed. Trailblazer? Sister, if this is trailblazing, I am the most cut-up, ill-equipped, whiny leader a team has ever encountered.

I frustratingly hack away at the brush that cuts me on this path of singleness, the thorns of lies that try to penetrate my skin, the leaves of worry, the vines of loneliness that weave so tight before my eyes that the only way I can even know there is a way forward is by the path at my feet. (And even that isn't so comforting because I don't know where it leads.)

"Thy Word is a lamp unto my feet and a light unto my path . . ." I sing in my head as the tears pour forth and I push forward on this trail.

I guess I never realized people were watching. I've never noticed the innocent young faces lined up behind me, watching the clearing process and then walking through the openings my toiling has created.

I never knew this was for them.

If that is the case, then maybe the days I have wrestled with my singleness and the God who knows and loves me through it all were so that others behind me would see and then know an easier path.

You, my friend, married or single, female or male, you are blazing a trail with your life for the younger women and men behind you. They will have their own overgrowth to challenge them, and they will lead the way for others.

Because you are making a way for them, saving them some pain that your bloodied arms prove is real, and honoring their footsteps by providing a clear path.

Never forget as you step forward with your life that you are a trailblazer.

Someone is watching.

It's the walking in front of. It's the standing beside. It's the trudging behind. We do this because we aren't alone in it. Even if you don't see others watching or standing or following, they are there. Women, young men, old men — all sorts of people. Seeing you be brave may be all they need to be brave. That may be all it takes.

You get the chance to live courageously. You were meant for it. You were born for it. It never feels easy, and it never is free. But it is what we want more than anything else.

This is your map. This is your story. Be brave for yourself, be brave for your God, and be brave for the onlookers, the ones who will be inspired by you to inspire others.

———

My dear friends Drew and Ellie Holcomb just played at
Bonnaroo for the first time. Bonnaroo is a huge outdoor
music festival in Manchester, Tennessee. To be asked to
play there is to say you have really made an impact musi-
cally on lots of lives. I asked Ellie how it went, and she said,
"It was incredible. A bucket list moment. It was everything
we dreamed it would be."

After years of working, of saying small, brave yeses
for their career — at first opening for other artists, all
the recording sessions, concert venues, and performance
opportunities — here they are saying a big yes. Their brave
is on a stage in front of all of us, and if you've heard any of
their music, you know it changes you and affects you. And
who knows where it goes from here.

I watch them. I observe their courage. I see the yeses
they say, and it builds something in me. It makes me want
to be brave with my art so others can be inspired. And the
courage trickles down and down and down to more people
than Drew and Ellie will ever know.

So you do it for them — for the people watching and for
the ones who will come behind you. But you do it for yourself too. You choose it because it's the way you want to live.

Everything hinges on courage. Absolutely everything.

And when you choose it, maybe I will too, and then the
dominos of cowardice will start to fall, and the sound we
hear as those dominoes in your mind crash to the ground
will be the sound of fear losing.

You want to change the world? Be brave. Be you. Don't
try to be someone else or do someone else's brave thing.

Don't move to Africa because it is brave. Move because it sounds like the most terrifyingly perfect next step for you. Don't write a song because it takes courage. Write it because you'll puke if you don't — even if you puke when you do. Because it matters. Every moment matters. And you being you? That is brave. It will make me brave. We will all be brave.

the rhythm

June 2013
My dining room table, Nashville, Tennessee

Some would say to be brave is to be mapless, the map crumpled up and thrown out the window, all willy-nilly drive until the car runs out of gas and then you figure out where you are. Though that may sound fun (to you), it has nothing to do with real courage. Does being brave mean being without boundary or constraint? Honestly, I don't think so. If you are brave, you are willing to walk the map that is yours, the one with twists and turns you've never expected, and you must be disciplined enough to stay on the narrow road under your feet. Step by step. Each step leads to the next, and before you know it, you are walking in a rhythm of courage.

I never tied discipline to courage. I never saw the correlation. I guess I should have, since I lack in both. But in all matters — physical, mental, and spiritual — I believe that to live a disciplined life leads to a brave life. We long

177

to be brave in the big moments, in the clutch times, in the times when our backs are up against a wall. But to get there? It's the everyday. It's the practice. It's the steps. It's the discipline.

Let's be real; that's not the most fun answer you've ever heard. None of us enjoy discipline. Hebrews 12:11 puts it perfectly: "No discipline seems pleasant at the time, but painful. Later on, however, it produces a harvest of righteousness and peace for those who have been trained by it."

And in *The Message*? Boom. "At the time, discipline isn't much fun. It always feels like it's going against the grain. Later, of course, it pays off handsomely, for it's the well-trained who find themselves mature in their relationship with God."

It always feels like it's going against the grain.

Yet. *It pays off handsomely.*

———

I decided to run a half marathon in the spring of 2010.

It was a ridiculous decision. I don't like running. I have never run that far — ever — and prior to that race, I was a consistent forty-five-minute 5Ker.

Do you know what that means?

I'm slow. Like, fifteen-minute mile slow.

And running a half marathon means going 13.1 miles at fifteen minutes a mile. You don't even have to do the math to realize that is a long time.

But my friends wanted to do it, and as you can imagine, I'm not great at saying no to anything social *and* it was a race in Seaside Beach, Florida, which happens to be one of my lifelong favorite places to go.

Here's what I had worked through in my mind: If I was going to be moving my body for 13.1 miles, I figured the beach was flat and being by the ocean was beautiful.

(Classic search for the path of least resistance.)

I signed up, paid my money, and booked my flight to Florida and was immediately full of regret. But the other girls — Blair, Katie, and Emily — had signed up, paid, and booked as well, so there was no backing out.

I downloaded a training program to my iPhone the fall before the race and decided I would spend six months really training for this half marathon.

I didn't.

(My hard stances on things really end up being more hilarious than anything, don't they?)

So by the time March rolled around and we were packing for the weekend, I had jogged approximately three miles in my training.

And I was about to attempt thirteen. And one-tenth.

———

The morning was cold, especially for the Florida coast in March. The race began, and about a quarter mile in, I had to start walking because my right calf was cramping up. My friends went ahead without me, which was great and expected. They were runners, and they had trained, you know, like a normal person in a race. My iPod kept me company as I walked/jogged/speed walked through the race route. The route, by the way — and spoiler alert — was not along the beach. It curved inland, and the road was flanked by mossy Florida trees and swamp. The edge of the road was covered in gloves, long-sleeve shirts, and other warm clothing items that people had just mindlessly discarded.

Mile 2 was the worst. I thought this was literally the worst decision I had ever made. For so early in the race, I was already feeling soreness creeping up my legs and was concerned I wasn't going to finish. But I kept going, mainly because my iPod was still playing the playlist I had designed specifically for this half marathon. On mile 8 I felt like a million bucks. I had turned the corner about a mile and a half before and was elated. It just felt like I was in the flow and all was well.

After more than three and a half hours, I crossed that finish line. Only three gift packs remained on the table, and in the official standings of thousands of racers, I finished next to last.

Three grandmas walking finished in front of me.

The next week was the most painful week of my life. Every muscle hurt. Every. Single. One. I walked like I had just ridden a horse from Maine to that very Florida beach. My underarms and other places (ahem) were chafed and scabbing. I pretty much just wanted to lie on the floor like a starfish, with an IV of ibuprofen for two or ten days.

My lack of training — and lack of discipline — really came back to haunt me after that race. And I'll tell you what, it'll be a long, long time before I sign up for a half marathon again. Hopefully never. I think I'm more of a 5K or 10K kind of girl, you know, the kind of racer who can finish in less time than it took the Titanic to sink.

———

I'd have done better in that race, dealt with less pain, and possibly been willing to attempt another race of that distance had I actually trained.

Discipline has always felt like rules to me, and even though I'm a natural-born rule follower, when I'm the one making the rules and trying to keep them, it's not as natural. The truth is that discipline isn't rules you have to live by or laws you have to obey; discipline is the work done on the practice field so you are ready for the big game.

I wasn't ready for the race because I didn't put in my time practicing.

Musicians practice. A lot. Ask anyone in Nashville who shares a wall or a house or a driveway or a garage with a musician — they know this all too well. Drummers? They ruin the neighborhood. Doctors practice. I'll never forget walking into my living room and seeing my roommate, a PA school student, sewing up stiff sponges. Practicing her stitches and her technique was hugely important. Now, doing an internship in Uganda, she is able to heal and save lives because of hours of practice on our couch. My pastor practices his entire sermon multiple times each week before he gives it, including at 6:30 a.m. on Sunday morning.

Professionals choose to practice, even when it hurts, because they know that practicing gives them the strength and power to perform in clutch moments.

"Practice makes perfect" is true. "Practice makes confidence" is truer.

If I had to pick one non-Trinity Bible character to have a crush on, it would totally be Benaiah. Do you know him? If he were alive today, I think he'd be a football player. And I have a very soft spot in my heart for a man in a football uniform.

First mentioned in 2 Samuel 23, Benaiah is one of David's mighty fighting men. That chapter talks of all the mighty exploits this strong man performed — killing a man seven and a half feet tall, killing two of Moab's strongest men, and fighting a lion in a pit on a snowy day.

Talk about the odds stacked against you.

A lion.

In a pit.

On a snowy day.

I don't even want to look a tiger in the eyes at the zoo. I can't imagine going head-to-head with a lion while trapped in a pit as snow made the terrain wet and slick and cold.

Benaiah went on to be the head of King David's bodyguards and the head of King Solomon's army as well.

He was a dude — a man's man in every sense of the word.

What the Bible doesn't talk about is Benaiah's training — the days and days of practice and healthy eating and building his body to become that kind of man. It took discipline and training to be able to go into that pit while knowing the challenges, and yet to have the confidence that he wouldn't lose.

The reason Benaiah didn't freak out in that pit, and freak out over the challenges that went along with it, is because he had done the training and all the day-to-day work that was necessary to get there.

How do you train for that kind of run-in? Yeah, I have no idea. But he did it.

Courage is like that, I think. Whether you are trying to finish a race or a book or that hard conversation you've been avoiding, the training leading up to that event is what makes it possible to face the fear and walk forward anyway.

Quit complaining about discipline and start seeing it as a powerful tool for courageous living.

———

We sat outside for summer Bible study, three adults and about thirty college students. Adam and Allison host, and the students show up in the summer like ants to a picnic. As we read through 2 Corinthians, we landed in a conversation about discipline. I wrinkled my nose like something smelled rotten — discipline was not my favorite topic. But as we talked, a word kept repeating — *rhythm*. "Get into a rhythm of discipline," a student said, talking about Bible reading, prayer, and the other pillars of our daily faith walk. "I bet it won't feel so hard anymore, huh? Because it doesn't sound like work, but like a rhythm we move to," another said. I was moved by the idea. That felt possible. Get in a rhythm. Practice the rhythms.

And then Jesus tells us of rhythms:

> "Are you tired? Worn out? Burned out on religion? Come to me. Get away with me and you'll recover your life. I'll show you how to take a real rest. Walk with me and work with me — watch how I do it. *Learn the unforced rhythms of grace.* I won't lay anything heavy or ill-fitting on you. Keep company with me and you'll learn to live freely and lightly."
>
> MATTHEW 11:28 – 30 MSG, emphasis added

Unforced rhythms of grace. Discipline as a rhythm. Could discipline look like grace and make me braver?

———

My friend Andrew Harris is a baseball player at Vanderbilt. Andrew is kind and respectful and always looks handsomely put together for church on Sunday. If he was in a beauty pageant, he would totally be Ms. Congeniality. Or Mr. Congeniality, as the case may be.

Andrew has been a member of the Vanderbilt baseball team every year of his college life, but he doesn't get a lot of playing time. There's no nice way to say it. He just doesn't. But he shows up to every practice. He shows up to work out and is a leader on the team. He practices like he's a starter and could get into any game at any moment. He feels just as invested in the success of the team as the center fielder who plays every inning of every game. And this kid? He loves baseball, and he loves his teammates. But he doesn't get to play.

When he came to Vanderbilt as a freshman, the hardest

season of his life had just happened. His mother died of cancer in the fall of his senior year of high school, and he had broken a vertebra in his back during the spring. His whole world was turned upside down, and things that were always going to be there were suddenly gone.

As he went to rehabilitation that fall as a college freshman, his frustration built. Nothing was going the way he had hoped. But one day, he felt like he heard God whisper to him about his purpose on that team. *What if my being here isn't about playing but about something bigger?* he thought.

He decided to go about his business. To be the best player he could be, whether or not that meant playing, and going to the field every day to prepare. Also, Andrew is great at having fun. So he had lots of fun.

This past spring, Andrew's senior season, Vanderbilt played incredibly, and I went to a game or so a week. I've watched a lot of college baseball in the last few years, far more than I ever did when I was an actual college student. College ministry will provide such opportunities.

And in all the games I've watched, I bet Andrew has been on the field fewer than five times. So in a season where they play sixty games, there's a minimum of three at bats per game for him. Of the two hundred possible at bats for Andrew, he's been up to the plate maybe five times.

I don't want the math to get you down, but that's a pretty low percentage.

But the day-in-and-day-out stuff of being on a team — training and disciplining his body, showing up — he's done it all.

In the last home game of the regular season, Vandy was in a hard-nosed battle with the University of Alabama, an SEC rival. They played tough and were looking good, but it was a really close game. In fact, they were in a situation where a sacrifice bunt was needed to move the runners forward.

Out of the dugout walks Andrew Harris.

The crowd cheers.

Andrew goes up to bat, and after a series of pitches that are a mix of balls and strikes, that man lays down a sacrifice bunt in the exact right way, a little hopper down the third-base line. The runners advance, and Andrew is thrown out at first base. (That's the goal, by the way — to move the other runners ahead to the next base, even if it means the hitter himself, Andrew in this case, is out. That's why they call it a sacrifice.)

It was perfect.

As Andrew turns to jog back to the dugout, the crowd erupts. People on their feet, yelling and cheering. He did the exact same thing in a real game that he had practiced a thousand times before.

He defeated that lion in a pit on a snowy day. His practice got him there — standing at home plate, called on in a clutch moment, and succeeding. The voice of fear was there, the pressure was on, and he nailed it. Absolutely nailed it.

And the crowd loved it.

———

Two weeks later, in the SEC tournament championship game, Andrew was called on again. When LSU, Vandy's opponent, saw who was coming out of the dugout to bat, they intentionally walked him.

They. Walked. Him.

How often do you see a pinch hitter get walked — especially one who rarely plays? I would never claim to know the ins and outs of why a coach makes a decision on whom to walk or whom to pitch to, but I can tell you what every Vandy fan in the stands thought.

LSU knew what was coming. A perfect bunter. And it wasn't a risk worth taking.

It was gratifying to see them afraid.

Brave Andrew. Going to practice every day, hustling every day, seldom playing. But when he does, when he gets to stand there at home plate and execute a play, he does it. Like Benaiah, when Andrew is in the clutch moment, the make-or-break moment, he's brave and confident and takes care of the job.

That week I called Andrew. We met at a local bagel place, and while he ate his breakfast, we chatted about discipline and courage and those two at-bat situations. Because I knew what I saw from the stands. I saw his discipline pay off, and I wanted to hear all about it.

He said every time he walks to the plate, he thinks about all the times he has done this play right in practice and every time it has worked on the field. He is full of confidence, even when the other team's fans are screaming their heads off. "The outside forces can cause anxiety, but discipline is what controls that. I know what I can do." He looks me right in the eyes when he says that, and I totally believe him.

He knows what he can do.

He knows the power behind the practice. The purpose behind the repetition. The gift of discipline.

It pays off handsomely.

———

The parallels are many. The ways we can see discipline and courage connect in our spiritual, mental, and physical lives are unlimited.

What does that discipline look like? I don't know for you. I just know that I often like to label discipline as something boring and unnecessary when really, if you want to be brave and be ready to be called into the game, you have to practice.

I'm never going to sacrifice bunt. I may love my Vandy baseball players, but they aren't asking me to suit up anytime soon. But when I see Andrew, I know I want to be like him.

I am a part of a nationwide teen girls' event called Girls of Grace. We travel and spend our Saturdays in cities around America teaching, worshiping, and hanging out with lots and lots of teen girls, their mothers, and their leaders. It's a full-day conference with speakers and bands and worship, and I absolutely love it. When I went to my first conference in 2012, I had never spoken in front of that many girls before. I had been speaking in front of teen audiences for a while at my church's youth group, local private school chapels, retreats, and camps. One event led to another, and within a few years, I was doing events outside of my community and speaking in front of larger crowds. But Girls of

Grace? It was the biggest deal. And I was so scared. Not only was I new to the team; I was saying some hard truths about how we should use our words.

I practiced my talk over and over again in front of the hotel bathroom mirror. I studied the Scriptures and made sure I had the translation I wanted to share. I timed myself as I stood there alone, to make sure I was on schedule. Like Andrew said, I also thought back to the other times I had spoken and brought them back to my memory. The confidence I had in God from those days I could call on here, and I did. The fear didn't stop me, though it was there, but practice and remembering God's faithfulness made me brave.

Discipline enables courage to show up.

It shows up when temptation feels like too much.

It shows up when the desire to quit is more than you can take.

It shows up when you get that middle of the night phone call from a friend in trouble.

It shows up.

Your discipline, the rhythm that makes you the best you — whether it's training your body, your mind, or your spirit — shows up when it is time to say the right thing, do the right thing, be the brave person you want to be. It's the practice that makes perfect, and the practice that makes you brave.

jesus

July 2013
Portland Brew, Nashville, Tennessee

I am thirty-three years old.

At this point, Jesus and I have lived on earth about the same amount of time, give or take. We both lived through our twenties — he with no mistakes or regrets, me with enough for both of us. Something gets very real about Jesus being human when you are the same age as him.

I've known Jesus since I was five years old, but I love him more today than I ever imagined I could as a little bitty thing.

We always went to church when I was a kid, at the time more out of obligation and the social norms for Georgia life in the 1980s than out of an actual passion or relationship. We attended First United Methodist Church in Marietta, where my mom was in the youth group in the 1960s and there was (is) a Sunday school classroom named after my grandfather. As a child, it was rare that I had to attend "big church." Sunday school was usually an hour well spent, but there were a few times when I sat with my parents in the large sanctuary.

I can probably show you which pew I was sitting in on that May Sunday in 1985. There was nothing unique or abnormal about that morning. I just remember our pastor, Charles Sineath, making some sort of altar call, though I don't remember the exact words he used. I remember the feeling — that push on my insides that I now know is the Holy Spirit — and I remember looking up at my mom and telling her, "I think I'm supposed to go down there."

I know it seems impossibly crazy that a then five-year-old could remember such clear details, but I do. I think God did that on purpose for me, for the days when things felt too hard or for those teen years when I just was never sure of myself or him, so I would always know that what I had decided on that day was true, even if everything else felt like shifting sand.

Mom and I walked forward, and I knelt on the red, padded cushion and leaned my little chest into the mahogany railing. Maybe my dad was there too? Pastor Sineath came down to me and asked me questions I don't remember word for word, but I knew I was asking Jesus to forgive me for doing bad things and to come into my heart and live there.

It was real. It was a decision I made. I knew God was real. I knew Jesus was God's Son. And I knew Jesus had died for me because I was a sinner.

My childhood years and teen years are just a plethora of stories cycloning around God and Jesus — reading the Bible and trying to understand it, being so involved at church that if the doors were open and the Coke machine was taking quarters, I was probably there. I saw God answer prayers, and I tried to love him as best I could.

I went to the University of Georgia and immediately got involved in the Wesley Foundation, a campus ministry run by the former youth pastor from FUMC. So yes, it was virtually the college version of my youth group — same leader and lots of the same students involved.

I went to the freshman Bible study, and to be honest, I kinda thought I was too mature to be there. I mean, I had been a Christian forever and I lived with my best friend (who was a junior), so it felt hard to relate to many of these college freshmen. It was old hat for me. I went to the Bible study mainly because I was supposed to, which by that point had become a big reason for a lot of the things I did in my faith. Because I did not really know life without being told to have quiet times and read your Bible and pray, it became just a big checklist that you go down day after day until you die.

Obviously I had a real understanding of what it is like to be in a relationship with the Lord. (Yeah, right.)

At that first freshman Bible study, I was put in a small group with a leader named Kimberly. One of the first questions she posed, which I was sure I'd be able to answer easily because, hello, I was the professional Christian here, was "How is your relationship with God different from your relationship with Jesus?"

Like an atomic bomb set off in the middle of the life I

had always known, that question blew up everything for me. I had never considered it. The Trinity—Father, Son, Holy Spirit—in my mind are all God (they are), but I did not ever think of them as individuals as well (they are). And that question changed everything for me.

I started to see Jesus as Jesus.

———

That may sound mystic and weird to think of the Father, Son, and Holy Spirit as three unique relationships, but I think that's part of the mystery of all of this—that they are three, but they are one. And if you look at the language throughout the Bible, God is our Father. We are described as the bride of Christ. The Holy Spirit is our counselor, our advocate. It's clear they are three distinct persons while sharing one essence.

But when you *only* think about Jesus as divine (which he is), then you sorta miss the fact that Jesus is human (which he is). So when my mind and heart began to reflect on the two natures a bit, everything changed. The things I read about Jesus changed. *Wait, he turned water into wine? Wait, he walked on water? A human? Wait, his friends turned on him—they slept when they should have prayed, pretended they didn't know him, sold him out in the most literal sense ever?*

And here we are. Both thirty-three. I can't imagine my friends turning on me the way Peter turned on Jesus. I can't imagine church leaders hating me the way they hated Jesus. I can't imagine being brave in all the ways he was. I can't imagine not knowing him. I'm so glad I get to. Something changed the closer I got to his age. I started to know him differently. I saw him like one of my friends, like one of the dudes I hang with all the time. He's not some adult doing adult things; he's my age.

It stokes my fires of courage, remembering that Jesus was human, that Jesus did some majorly brave things right here—right where I am. Single like me. Thirty-three like me. Human like me. Sinless, unlike me, but tempted like me.

And he took a risk on me.

———

At this point, you've realized I'm not always great at this. "This?" This being life. So for another human like Jesus to bank on me seems a bit unwise. He knows I'm a screwup, and for that, he gave his life. I am so grateful for that salvation. But over and over again, I ask Jesus for forgiveness and rescue, and he always provides them. You would never buy a car that got a flat tire every time you test-drove it, and you would stop eating at restaurants that repeatedly got your order wrong. And yet, Jesus does that for me all the time. I have a flat tire and get his order wrong and sin and everything in between. He risks for me, and he risks on me.

———

Courage was born on Christmas Day.

The truth of who Jesus is and what he did on earth— the Son of God who came to earth to take on our sins—is the most courageous thing this planet has ever seen.

I recently heard Andy Byrd, a teacher at the YWAM Circuit Rider School, say, "Jesus fasted from heaven for thirty-three years." And it broke my heart. I guess I had never considered all that Jesus gave up — I mean, I knew he laid aside the glory he had with the Father and I knew he took on human flesh, but I guess I forgot he gave up freedom from temptation. He gave up being worshiped and adored and fully loved by everyone around him. He gave up all the things you dream heaven could be like.

As if that wasn't enough, for those thirty-three years on earth he healed and set free and forgave sins and poured love into those around him.

Then. He died on the cross, taking away our sins and bringing us salvation.

Then. He was resurrected so we could have eternal life and be set free from the guilt of sin.

"Jesus paid it all, all to him I owe; sin had left a crimson stain, he washed it white as snow."*

That is courage.

While it is important to celebrate bravery in others and call it forth in ourselves, it would be ridiculous to believe that anything we do can hold a candle to the courageous things Jesus did for us.

> Think of yourselves the way Christ Jesus thought of himself. He had equal status with God but didn't think so much of himself that he had to cling to the advantages of that status no matter what. Not at all. When the time came, he set aside the privileges of deity and took on the status of a slave, became *human*! Having become human, he stayed human. It was an

---

*"Jesus Paid It All," lyrics by Elvina M. Hall, 1865. Public domain.

incredibly humbling process. He didn't claim special privileges. Instead, he lived a selfless, obedient life and then died a selfless, obedient death — and the worst kind of death at that: a crucifixion.

Because of that obedience, God lifted him high and honored him far beyond anyone or anything, ever, so that all created beings in heaven and on earth — even those long ago dead and buried — will bow in worship before this Jesus Christ, and call out in praise that he is the Master of all, to the glorious honor of God the Father.

PHILIPPIANS 2:5 – 11 MSG

Right? Brave.
I love him.

good-bye

July 2013
My front porch, Nashville, Tennessee

My last Sunday in Scotland was November 20, 2011. I flew out on November 21, which made perfect sense to me because 21 is my favorite number and it is 7 + 7 + 7. Completion. And that's how it felt. It felt finished.

At our last team brunch on that Sunday, I asked God if I was different. I asked him if I had been and done all that he wanted. And I had the most grateful heart. For my friends in that room — for Esther and Harry, Leisa, Tom and Leigh Ann, James, Melissa, Kenneth; for the students at Crossroads Church; for the realization that this lifelong dream had become my reality; for all the ways I saw God there.

And Melissa began singing a worship song derived from a proclamation of the Moravian missionaries Johann Leonhard Dober and David Nitschmann in 1732, who sold themselves into slavery to bring the gospel to the West Indies islands: "May the Lamb that was slain receive the reward of His suffering!" and then she sings, "starting with me!"

And my heart rose to meet that.

Making the brave choice in your life is going to change the world. At the least, it will change your world. But I dare not limit what you are going to do on this planet, friend. Your life is Jesus' reward for his suffering — your brave yeses, your courageous noes, hanging on, letting go, going there, staying here, all of it.

I hope you've already done it. I hope you've already taken that first step because I am sure, like I've rarely been so sure of anything before, that your people are waiting and your God is watching with expectancy for you to see where your map is going to take you.

And today I pray peace for you.

Because even in the scariest moments, even when the map seems upside down or you can't see far enough ahead to feel brave enough to take a step, Jesus promises you peace: "Peace I leave with you; my peace I give you. I do not give to you as the world gives. Do not let your hearts be troubled and do not be afraid" (John 14:27).

So I pray peace for you, fellow traveler. We are embarking on something new today as we say good-bye, and I pray you will never be the same because of what Jesus has done in your heart. You are stronger than you know. You are more generous than you've allowed yourself to be. You are impacting the people around you far more than you realize.

Will you now also be brave? I promise you I will try. I am trying in relationship and in heart and in profession to live bravely and put fear out to pasture. Watch me try and fail and pull strength from it. Because I'm watching others and pulling strength from them too. I have many more stories I could share of people in my world who are courageous — moms and teens and single dudes and musicians and artists and my family and friends. But instead, I will say good-bye and hope and pray the best for you. I can only watch as you untie your ship from the dock, and I will give it enough of a shove that if you reached back, I couldn't grab your hand.

Instead, hold your map and the hand of your Father. And let's all be brave.

thank you

To my friends and family at Zondervan —
you have made so many of my dreams come true. Carolyn
McCready, what you have done with this book is miraculous and could just make me feel weepy. I am so thankful.
Dirk Buursma, your voice was the missing piece this book
needed to become whole. Thank you from the bottom of my
heart. Kyle Olund, your constant support is so appreciated.
Londa Alderink, thanks for creating a wide space for us to
grow this dream.

To my friends and family who have intentionally
stepped into this career with me — Kyle Chowning, Keith
Bordeaux, Kelli Haywood, Brian Smith, Adam Edelstein,
Leigh Holt, David Breen, Connor Harrell, Sarah Rademaker,
the Girls of Grace staff and team, Word Entertainment,
Dayspring and (in)courage writers, Mocha Club staff, Pete
Wilson, Jenni Catron, Stephen Brewster. On days when I'm
not sure, you are the ones who remind me why we are here.
I won't forget your kindness and how you each, in one way
or another, have held me up during the writing of this book.

Corene Israel, thank you for believing in my writing first. Seth Godin, thank you for teaching me to be brave enough to fail. I'll always have another idea.

To my friends and family in Marietta, Georgia — thank you for molding and shaping and holding me for so many years. I am here because of your investment, compassion, and support.

To my friends and family in Athens, Georgia — thank you for teaching me to be free and to be brave. Those years will always be some of the best. The impact the Wesley Foundation had on my life cannot be measured on this side of heaven, and I will always be grateful for that ministry. I hope that is reflected well here.

To my friends and family in Edinburgh, Scotland — thank you for making me one of your own. My heart lives with you in a way I don't know how to express.

To my friends and family in Nashville, Tennessee — thank you for loving me and showing me who I want to be. I'm a better me because of each of you.

To my friends who write — you inspire me.

To my friends who read — thank you for allowing me to continue to do this.

To Jesus — when I had nothing left, I had you. And you are more than enough. I love you with all my heart.

sounds good to me

As I wrote *Let's All Be Brave*, I listened to the following musicians/albums. I cannot recommend these artists enough. They are doing the hard work to make art that impacts the world. I am grateful. Buy their albums.

Brideshead Revisited
  soundtrack

Delirious?

The Lumineers

The Cinematic Orchestra

for KING & COUNTRY

Elenowen

Ingrid Michaelson

All Sons & Daughters

The Wedding Band

Beasts of the Southern Wild
  soundtrack

Taylor Swift

Andrew Ripp

Adam Agin

Meredith Andrews

Lady Antebellum

Steven Curtis Chapman

Ellie Holcomb

Matt Wertz

She & Him

Foster the People

The Civil Wars

Dave Barnes

Jon Foreman

Johnnyswim